9

In this section

The return to Jerusalem
The rebuilding of the Temple
The roles played by Ezra and Nehemiah
Esther's prevention of a massacre

The Lord's return

Two buildings near the Temple
Ezekiel 42:1–14

Measurements of the Temple area
Ezekiel 42:15–20

The Lord returns to the Temple
Ezekiel 43:1–12

The Altar
Ezekiel 43:13–17

Consecration of Altar
Ezekiel 43:18–27

Use of the East Gate
Ezekiel 44:1–3

Rules for admission to Temple
Ezekiel 44:4–9

The Levites are excluded
Ezekiel 44:10–14

The priests
Ezekiel 44:15–31

Ezekiel 43:1–9

**1Then the man brought me to the
gate facing east, 2and I saw the
glory of the God of Israel coming
from the east. His voice was like
the roar of rushing waters, and the
land was radiant with his glory.
3The vision I saw was like the
vision I had seen when he came
to destroy the city and like the
visions I had seen by the Kebar
River, and I fell face down. 4The
glory of the Lord entered the tem-
ple through the gate facing east.
5Then the Spirit lifted me up and
brought me into the inner court,
and the glory of the Lord filled
the temple.**

**6While the man was standing
beside me, I heard someone
speaking to me from inside the
temple. 7He said: "Son of man, this
is the place of my throne and the
place for the soles of my feet. This
is where I will live among the
Israelites for ever. The house of
Israel will never again defile my
holy name – neither they nor their
kings – by their prostitution and
the lifeless idols of their kings at
their high places. ...**

For Thought and **Contemplation**

Make a point today of reflecting that, in these New Testament times, God's glory does not dwell in temples made with hands, but in the hearts of those who truly own Him as Lord. Are you one of them?

"Do you not know that your body is a temple of the Holy Spirit, who is in you, whom you have received from God? You are not your own; you were bought at a price. Therefore honour God with your body." (1 Cor. 6:19–20)

WEEK 36

700 BC — *Assyrians besiege Jerusalem* — Nahum — Zephaniah — Josiah — Nebuchadnezzar — Jeremiah — Habakkuk — Daniel taken to Babylon — 600 BC — FALL OF JUDAH — Ezekiel — Jerusalem destroyed — Exile in Babylon

Temple worship

DAY **246**

Ezekiel 45:1–6

**[1]"'When you allot the land as an
inheritance, you are to present to
the Lord a portion of the land as a
sacred district, 25,000 cubits long
and 20,000 cubits wide; the entire
area will be holy. [2]Of this, a section
500 cubits square is to be for the
sanctuary, with 50 cubits around
it for open land. [3]In the sacred
district, measure off a section
25,000 cubits long and 10,000
cubits wide. In it will be the
sanctuary, the Most Holy Place.
[4]It will be the sacred portion of the
land for the priests, who minister
in the sanctuary and who draw
near to minister before the Lord.
It will be a place for their houses
as well as a holy place for the
sanctuary. [5]An area 25,000 cubits
long and 10,000 cubits wide will
belong to the Levites, who serve
in the temple, as their possession
for towns to live in.
[6]You are to give the city as its
property an area 5,000 cubits
wide and 25,000 cubits long,
adjoining the sacred portion; it
will belong to the whole house
of Israel.' "**

The Lord's portion of the land
Ezekiel 45:1–6

The prince's portion
Ezekiel 45:7–8

Weights and measures
Ezekiel 45:9–15

The prince's duty
Ezekiel 45:16–17

The Festivals
Ezekiel 45:18–25

Rules regarding worship
Ezekiel 46:1–12

The daily offering
Ezekiel 46:13–15

The prince's land
Ezekiel 46:16–18

Place for boiling the offerings
Ezekiel 46:19–24

The stream flowing from the Temple
Ezekiel 47:1–12

For Thought and **Contemplation**

"Where do you worship?" asked one Christian of another. The reply he got quite startled him. "I worship in Woolworth's, in the High Street, in the bus, in the train, in the office, in my house … anywhere and everywhere." If you can't worship God everywhere, then you won't worship Him anywhere.

"God is spirit, and his worshippers must worship in spirit and in truth." (Jn. 4:24)

Zerubbabel and main party return
500 BC
Iron Age begins in Britain
Ezra returns
Malachi
400 BC
Cyrus
Zechariah Haggai
2nd Temple built
Nehemiah rebuilds walls of Jerusalem

The land's boundaries
Ezekiel 47:13–23

Division of land among the tribes
Ezekiel 48:1–9

The priests' and Levites' section
Ezekiel 48:10–20

The prince's section
Ezekiel 48:21–22

Land for the other tribes
Ezekiel 48:23–29

The gates of Jerusalem
Ezekiel 48:30–35

More prophecy against Egypt
Ezekiel 29:17–21, 30:1–19

Ezekiel 48:30–35

**30"These will be the exits of the
city: Beginning on the north side,
which is 4,500 cubits long, 31the
gates of the city will be named
after the tribes of Israel. The three
gates on the north side will be the
gate of Reuben, the gate of Judah
and the gate of Levi.
32On the east side, which is 4,500
cubits long, will be three gates:
the gate of Joseph, the gate of
Benjamin and the gate of Dan.
33On the south side, which
measures 4,500 cubits, will be
three gates: the gate of Simeon,
the gate of Issachar and the gate
of Zebulun.
34On the west side, which is 4,500
cubits long, will be three gates:
the gate of Gad, the gate
of Asher and the gate of Naphtali.
35The distance all around will be
18,000 cubits.
And the name of the city from
that time on will be:
THE LORD IS THERE."**

For Thought and **Contemplation**

In the divine order of things, worship must always precede work. First comes God's command to worship, then the command to divide and resettle the land. Which takes precedence in your life? Work, or worship? We are worshippers first and workers second. Reverse the order and you will end up spiritually bankrupt.

"Therefore, I urge you, brothers, in view of God's mercy, to offer your bodies as living sacrifices, holy and pleasing to God – this is your spiritual act of worship." (Rom. 12:1)

WEEK 36

700 BC | *Assyrians besiege Jerusalem* | Nahum Zephaniah Josiah Nebuchadnezzar | 600 BC | Daniel taken to Babylon | Jeremiah Habakkuk | Jerusalem destroyed | FALL OF JUDAH | Ezekiel | Exile in Babylon

God's dealings with Nebuchadnezzar — DAY **248**

Daniel 4:34–37

**34 At the end of that time, I,
Nebuchadnezzar, raised my eyes
towards heaven, and my sanity
was restored. Then I praised the
Most High; I honoured and
glorified him who lives for ever.
His dominion is an eternal
dominion;
his kingdom endures from
generation to generation.
35 All the peoples of the earth
are regarded as nothing.
He does as he pleases
with the powers of heaven
and the peoples of the earth.
No-one can hold back his hand
or say to him: "What have you
done?"
36 At the same time that my sanity
was restored, my honour and
splendour were returned to me
for the glory of my kingdom. My
advisers and nobles sought me
out, and I was restored to my
throne and became even greater
than before. 37 Now I, Nebuchad-
nezzar, praise and exalt and glorify
the King of heaven, because
everything he does is right and all
his ways are just. And those who
walk in pride he is able to humble.**

Nebuchadnezzar's second dream
Daniel 4:4–18

Daniel's explanation
Daniel 4:19–27

Nebuchadnezzar's seven years of madness
Daniel 4:28–33

Death of Jeremiah 570 BC

Nebuchadnezzar is restored and praises God
Daniel 4:34–37

Release of Jehoiachin
2 Kings 25:27–30, Jeremiah 52:31–34

Daniel's vision of the four beasts
Daniel 7:1–8

His vision of the eternal God
Daniel 7:9–14

For Thought and **Contemplation**

How true is the Scripture that says: "Pride goes before destruction, a haughty spirit before a fall" (Proverbs 16:18). Lucifer's pride cost him his place in heaven, and the prospect of eternal judgment. Nebuchadnezzar's pride cost him his throne for seven years. How much is pride costing you?

"... That is why Scripture says: 'God opposes the proud but gives grace to the humble.' Submit yourselves, then, to God. Resist the devil, and he will flee from you." (Jas. 4:6–7)

Zerubbabel and main party return — *Iron Age begins in Britain* — Ezra returns — Malachi

500 BC — 400 BC

Cyrus — Zechariah Haggai, 2nd Temple built — Nehemiah rebuilds walls of Jerusalem

DAY **249** Psalms of the captivity

Psalm 123:1–4

1 I lift up my eyes to you,
to you whose throne is in heaven.
2 As the eyes of slaves look to the hand of their master,
as the eyes of a maid look to the hand of her mistress,
so our eyes look to the Lord our God,
till he shows us his mercy.
3 Have mercy on us, O Lord, have mercy on us,
for we have endured much contempt.
4 We have endured much ridicule from the proud,
much contempt from the arrogant.

For Thought and **Contemplation**

Some of the greatest psalms came out of the greatest distresses. Are you in distress at this moment. Then follow the example of the psalmists who, though they began by focusing on their problems, finished by focusing on God. This will help you, too, to turn your pain into a paean of praise.

"God is our refuge and strength, an ever-present help in trouble. ... The Lord Almighty is with us; the God of Jacob is our fortress." (Psa. 46:1 & 11)

WEEK 36

Nahum Zephaniah Josiah Nebuchadnezzar Jerusalem destroyed
700 BC | 600 BC | FALL OF JUDAH
Assyrians besiege Jerusalem Daniel taken to Babylon Ezekiel
Jeremiah Habakkuk Exile in Babylon

The Two Covenants

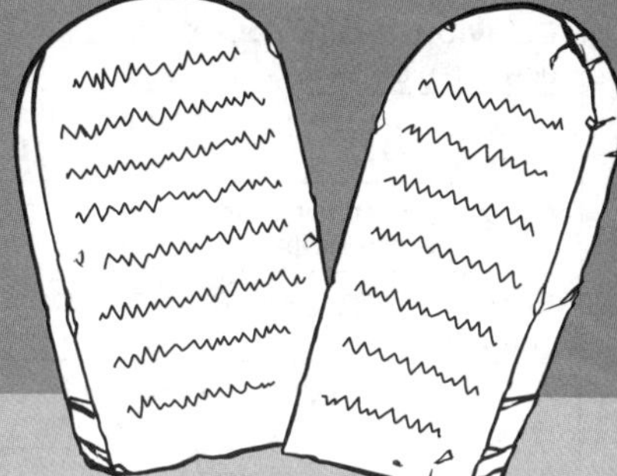

The old covenant

a. It was mediated by Moses (Ex. 19; Jn. 1:17; Gal. 3:19)

b. It was conditional (Deut. 28)

c. It could not produce righteousness (Heb. 8:8)

d. It was written on stone tablets (Ex. 32:15)

The new covenant

a. Mediated by Christ (Heb. 9:15; Jn. 1:17)

b. It is unconditional (Heb. 8:9)

c. It can produce the necessary righteousness (Heb. 8:11)

d. It is written on living hearts (Heb. 8:10)

DAY 250 The judgment of Babylon

Babylon's fall prophesied
Jeremiah 50:9–16

Israel's return prophesied
Jeremiah 50:17–20

God's judgment on Babylon
Jeremiah 50:21–46

Further judgment on Babylon
Jeremiah 51:1–14

A hymn of praise to God
Jeremiah 51:15–19

The Lord's hammer
Jeremiah 51:20–23

Babylon's punishment
Jeremiah 51:24–35

Jeremiah 50:17–20

17 "Israel is a scattered flock
that lions have chased away.
The first to devour him
was the king of Assyria;
the last to crush his bones
was Nebuchadnezzar king of Babylon."
18 Therefore this is what the Lord Almighty, the God of Israel, says:
"I will punish the king of Babylon and his land
as I punished the king of Assyria.
19 But I will bring Israel back to his own pasture
and he will graze on Carmel and Bashan;
his appetite will be satisfied
on the hills of Ephraim and Gilead.
20 In those days, at that time,"
declares the Lord,
"search will be made for Israel's guilt,
but there will be none,
and for the sins of Judah,
but none will be found,
for I will forgive the remnant I spare."

For Thought and **Contemplation**

Ever found yourself wondering why God allows sin and godlessness such freedom? Then remind yourself also of this – that every nation that rises up against God will one day fall. What happened to Babylon will happen to the godless nations of our own day. Learn to be patient with the patience of God.

"Blessed is the man who does not walk in the counsel of the wicked or stand in the way of sinners or sit in the seat of mockers. But his delight is in the law of the Lord, and on his law he meditates day and night." (Psa. 1:1–2)

WEEK 36

Nahum Zephaniah Josiah Nebuchadnezzar Jerusalem destroyed
700 BC | 600 BC | FALL OF JUDAH
Assyrians besiege Jerusalem Daniel taken to Babylon Ezekiel
Jeremiah Habakkuk Exile in Babylon

Daniel 5:13–16

[13]So Daniel was brought before the king, and the king said to him, "Are you Daniel, one of the exiles my father the king brought from Judah? [14]I have heard that the spirit of the gods is in you and that you have insight, intelligence and outstanding wisdom. [15]The wise men and enchanters were brought before me to read this writing and tell me what it means, but they could not explain it. [16]Now I have heard that you are able to give interpretations and to solve difficult problems. If you can read this writing and tell me what it means, you will be clothed in purple and have a gold chain placed around your neck, and you will be made the third highest ruler in the kingdom."

For Thought and **Contemplation**

There are three occasions in Scripture when God wrote with His finger a special message to men. Can you think of them? One, of course, is found here in the story of Belshazzar's feast. The other two can be found in Exodus 31:18 and John 8:6. Look them up right now.

"'This is the covenant I will make with them after that time, says the Lord. I will put my laws in their hearts, and I will write them on their minds.' Then he adds: 'Their sins and lawless acts I will remember no more.'" (Heb. 10:16-17)

Zerubbabel and main party return
500 BC
Iron Age begins in Britain
Ezra returns
Malachi
400 BC
Cyrus
Zechariah Haggai
2nd Temple built
Nehemiah rebuilds walls of Jerusalem

DAY **252** The command to rebuild the Temple

Daniel's prayer
Daniel 9:1–19

Gabriel's explanation
Daniel 9:20–27

The prayer of a troubled young man
Psalm 102:1–28

People challenged to rebuild the Temple
Ezra 5:13, 2 Chronicles 36:22–23, Ezra 1:1–4

A prayer for deliverance
Psalm 126:1–6

A prayer for the nation's welfare
Psalm 85:1–13

The people's response to the challenge
Ezra 1:5–6

Ezra 1:1–4

**1 In the first year of Cyrus king of
Persia, in order to fulfil the word of
the Lord spoken by Jeremiah, the
Lord moved the heart of Cyrus
king of Persia to make a procla-
mation throughout his realm and
to put it in writing:
2 "This is what Cyrus king of Persia
says:
'The Lord, the God of heaven, has
given me all the kingdoms of the
earth and he has appointed me to
build a temple for him at
Jerusalem in Judah. 3 Anyone of his
people among you – may his God
be with him, and let him go up to
Jerusalem in Judah and build the
temple of the Lord, the God of
Israel, the God who is in
Jerusalem. 4 And the people of any
place where survivors may now
be living are to provide him with
silver and gold, with goods and
livestock, and with freewill
offerings for the temple of God
in Jerusalem.'"**

For Thought and **Contemplation**

If there is one truth that is underlined in reading through the Old Testament, it is the truth of God's great patience and everlasting mercy. Though time and time again He is disappointed with His people, He does not cast them off. And what He was He is, and always will be. Hallelujah!

"But because of his great love for us, God, who is rich in mercy, made us alive with Christ even when we were dead in transgressions – it is by grace you have been saved." (Eph. 2:4–5)

a bird's eye view of **Ezra & Nehemiah**

Place in the Bible	Main Characters	Special Features
Fifteenth and sixteenth Old Testament books; tenth and eleventh books of history.	Ezra, Nehemiah	In fulfilment of God's promise some Jews return to Jerusalem to rebuild the Temple. Later, Ezra calls the community to wholehearted obedience to God's laws, and Nehemiah, 14 years afterward, leads the rebuilding of the city walls.

Daniel in the lions' den

Daniel 6:25–28

25Then King Darius wrote to
all the peoples, nations and men
of every language throughout
the land:
"May you prosper greatly!
26I issue a decree that in every
part of my kingdom people must
fear and reverence the God
of Daniel.
For he is the living God
and he endures for ever;
his kingdom will not be destroyed,
his dominion will never end.
27He rescues and he saves;
he performs signs and wonders
in the heavens and on the earth.
He has rescued Daniel
from the power of the lions."
28So Daniel prospered during the
reign of Darius and the reign of
Cyrus the Persian.

The Temple's vessels returned
Ezra 1:7–11, 5:14–16

Cyrus' decree
Ezra 6:3–5

Daniel thrown to the lions
Daniel 6:1–18

His deliverance and its result
Daniel 6:19–28

Daniel's three weeks of mourning
Daniel 10:1–3

His vision by the River Tigris
Daniel 10:4–20

Revelation promised
Daniel 10:21

Revelation of future kingdom
Daniel 11:2–4

For Thought and **Contemplation**

You may not have to face the prospect of spending a night in a lions' den, but no doubt you have encountered that "roaring lion" who goes about "looking for someone to devour" (1 Pet. 5:8). Take heart – what God did for Daniel, He will do for you.

"... in all these things we are more than conquerors through him who loved us." (Rom. 8:37)

Jesus and the Books

Nehemiah faced ridicule and great opposition as he rebuilt Jerusalem. Jesus' followers too must expect opposition: "Blessed are you when people insult you, persecute you and falsely say all kinds of evil against you because of me" (Matt. 5:11).

Teaching

Ezra and Nehemiah are about building for God. Ezra the priest teaches the returned exiles about true worship, holiness and entire obedience to God. Nehemiah is an example of how diligent work and constant prayer go hand in hand in God's service.

A Verse to Remember

"'Blessed be your glorious name, and may it be exalted above all blessing and praise. You alone are the Lord. You made the heavens, ... the earth ... the seas ... You give life to everything, and the multitudes of heaven worship you.'" (Neh. 9:5–6)

The end times

The kingdoms of Egypt and Syria
Daniel 11:5–20

The evil king of Syria
Daniel 11:21–24

He will invade Egypt
Daniel 11:25–30

Remnant returns (49,897) 536 BC

The abomination that causes desolation
Daniel 11:31–35

Prophecy of the Antichrist
Daniel 11:36–39

His final hour
Daniel 11:40–45

The end times
Daniel 12:1–13

The list of the returning exiles: the men of Israel
Ezra 2:1–20

Those from various towns
Ezra 2:21–35

The priests
Ezra 2:36–39

Daniel 11:36–39

36"The king will do as he pleases. He will exalt and magnify himself above every god and will say unheard-of things against the God of gods. He will be successful until the time of wrath is completed, for what has been determined must take place. 37He will show no regard for the gods of his fathers or for the one desired by women, nor will he regard any god, but will exalt himself above them all.
38Instead of them, he will honour a god of fortresses; a god unknown to his fathers he will honour with gold and silver, with precious stones and costly gifts. 39He will attack the mightiest fortresses with the help of a foreign god and will greatly honour those who acknowledge him. He will make them rulers over many people and will distribute the land at a price."

For Thought and **Contemplation**

Someone has pointed out that Daniel is one of the few people in the Bible about whom nothing negative is written. What was the secret of his wonderful life? There are many reasons, not the least being his prowess in prayer. Are you satisfied with your prayer life? If not, then decide now to do something positive about it.

"This is the confidence we have in approaching God: that if we ask anything according to his will, he hears us. And if we know that he hears us – whatever we ask – we know that we have what we asked of him."
(1 Jn. 5:14–15)

WEEK 37

Zerubbabel and main party return | *Iron Age begins in Britain* | Ezra returns | Malachi

500 BC | 400 BC

Cyrus | Zechariah Haggai | 2nd Temple built | Nehemiah rebuilds walls of Jerusalem

The Return

DURING THE FIRST YEAR of Cyrus' reign in Babylon (539 BC), he issued the decree which permitted the Jews to return and rebuild the temple at Jerusalem.

Jeremiah had predicted the length of the captivity (see Jeremiah 25:11, 12; 29:10).

Isaiah had prophesied, 170 years before, that Cyrus would act in this way. (See Isa. 44:28; 45:1.)

There were three separate returns by the Jewish remnant: Zerubbabel led the first in 536 BC; Ezra led the second in 458 BC; and Nehemiah led the third in 445 BC.

In 535 BC the construction of the Temple began but it faced bitter opposition and so the prophets Haggai and Zechariah ministered to the discouraged remnant.

Nehemiah checks the list

The Levites, singers and gatekeepers
Ezra 2:40–42

The Temple servants and children of Solomon's servants
Ezra 2:43–58

No proof of ancestry
Ezra 2:59–63

The exiles' arrival at the Temple
Ezra 2:64–70

Nehemiah checks the family records
Nehemiah 7:5–7

Another list of the exiles
Nehemiah 7:8–69

Many contribute to the cost of restoring the Temple
Nehemiah 7:70–72

List of priests and Levites
Nehemiah 12:1–23

Assignment of duties
Nehemiah 12:24–26

Nehemiah 7:5–18

**5 So my God put it into my heart to
assemble the nobles, the officials
and the common people for
registration by families. I found the
genealogical record of those who
had been the first to return. This
is what I found written there:
6 These are the people of the
province who came up from the
captivity of the exiles whom
Nebuchadnezzar king of Babylon
had taken captive (they returned
to Jerusalem and Judah, each to
his own town, 7 in company with
Zerubbabel, Jeshua, Nehemiah,
Azariah, Raamiah, Nahamani,
Mordecai, Bilshan, Mispereth,
Bigvai, Nehum and Baanah):
The list of the men of Israel:**

8 the descendants of Parosh	**2,172**
9 of Shephatiah	**372**
10 of Arah	**652**
11 of Pahath-Moab (through the line of Jeshua and Joab)	**2,818**
12 of Elam	**1,254**
13 of Zattu	**845**
14 of Zaccai	**760**
15 of Binnui	**648**
16 of Bebai	**628**
17 of Azgad	**2,322**
18 of Adonikam	**667 ...**

For Thought and **Contemplation**

Nehemiah made certain that all who came to live in Jerusalem were there by divine right – hence the painstaking procedure of checking every name. How will it be with you when the time comes for you to enter the "New Jerusalem"? Is your name written there?

"... do not rejoice that the spirits submit to you, but rejoice that your names are written in heaven." (Lk. 10:20)

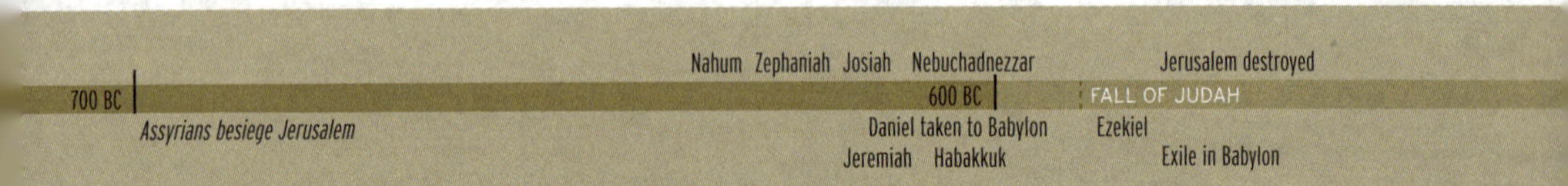

Rebuilding programme begins

Ezra 3:10–13

**10When the builders laid the foun-
dation of the temple of the Lord,
the priests in their vestments and
with trumpets, and the Levites
(the sons of Asaph) with cymbals,
took their places to praise the
Lord, as prescribed by David king
of Israel. 11With praise and thanks-
giving they sang to the Lord:
"He is good;
his love to Israel endures for ever."
And all the people gave a great
shout of praise to the Lord,
because the foundation of the
house of the Lord was laid. 12But
many of the older priests and
Levites and family heads, who had
seen the former temple, wept
aloud when they saw the founda-
tion of this temple being laid, while
many others shouted for joy. 13No-
one could distinguish the sound
of the shouts of joy from the
sound of weeping, because the
people made so much noise. And
the sound was heard far away.**

The exiles rebuild the altar
Ezra 3:1–7

In praise of Jerusalem
Psalm 87:1–7

Rebuilding of the Temple begins
Ezra 3:8–9

The priests and Levites praise the Lord
Ezra 3:10–13

Longing for God's house
Psalm 84:1–12

In praise of God's goodness
Psalm 107:1–43

A song of praise and thanksgiving
Psalm 66:1–20

For Thought and **Contemplation**

The first thing the children of Israel did when they returned to Jerusalem was to build an altar. Worship, they realised, must come before work. Make a list of the things you have to do today, and before you do them, commit each item to God. You will find life runs better this way.

"Come, let us bow down in worship, let us kneel before the Lord our Maker; for he is our God and we are the people of his pasture, the flock under his care." (Psa. 95:6–7)

WEEK 37

Zerubbabel and main party return · 500 BC · *Iron Age begins in Britain* · Ezra returns · Malachi · 400 BC

Cyrus · Zechariah · Haggai · 2nd Temple built · Nehemiah rebuilds walls of Jerusalem

DAY **257**

Opposition to the work

Samaritan interference
Ezra 4:1–5

The security of God's people
Psalm 125:1–5

Letters of accusation
Ezra 4:6–16

Artaxerxes' answer
Ezra 4:17–22

Work suspended for seven years
Ezra 4:23–24

A prayer against Israel's enemies
Psalm 129:1–8

Haggai and Zechariah
Ezra 5:1

People reproached for neglect of Temple
Haggai 1:1–10

Zerubbabel and Joshua
Ezra 5:2, Haggai 1:11–15

The splendour of the future Temple
Haggai 2:1–9

Zechariah's plea
Zechariah 1:1–6

Psalm 125:1–5

1 Those who trust in the Lord are like Mount Zion,
which cannot be shaken but endures for ever.
2 As the mountains surround Jerusalem,
so the Lord surrounds his people
both now and for evermore.
3 The sceptre of the wicked will not remain
over the land allotted to the righteous,
for then the righteous might use
their hands to do evil.
4 Do good, O Lord, to those who are good,
to those who are upright in heart.
5 But those who turn to crooked ways
the Lord will banish with the evildoers.
Peace be upon Israel.

For Thought and **Contemplation**

No work of God is ever established without opposition. Perhaps you are finding this to be true in your own life at this very moment. Be encouraged; opposition may seem to work against you – but it really works *for* you. It makes you less dependent on yourself and more dependent on God.

"But the Lord stood at my side and gave me strength, so that through me the message might be fully proclaimed and all the Gentiles might hear it. And I was delivered from the lion's mouth." (2 Timothy 4:17)

a bird's eye view of **Haggai & Zechariah**

Place in the Bible

Thirty-seventh and thirty-eighth Old Testament books; fifteenth and sixteenth books of prophecy.

Jesus and the Books

Haggai was clear that the Lord has chosen the Jews to be His people, just as Christ called and chose people to be His followers: "You did not choose me, but I chose you ..." (John 15:16).
Zechariah has numerous references

Zechariah's visions

Zechariah 4:6–10

**6So he said to me, "This is the
word of the Lord to Zerubbabel:
'Not by might nor by power, but by
my Spirit,' says the Lord Almighty.
7What are you, O mighty moun-
tain? Before Zerubbabel you will
become level ground. Then he will
bring out the capstone to shouts
of 'God bless it! God bless it!'"
8Then the word of the Lord came
to me: 9"The hands of Zerubbabel
have laid the foundation of this
temple; his hands will also com-
plete it. Then you will know that
the Lord Almighty has sent me
to you.
10Who despises the day of small
things? Men will rejoice when they
see the plumb-line in the hand of
Zerubbabel.
(These seven are the eyes of
the Lord, which range throughout
the earth.)"**

Haggai confronts the priests
Haggai 2:10–14

The Lord promises blessing
Haggai 2:15–23

Zechariah's vision of the horses
Zechariah 1:7–17

God's promise to Zerubbabel
Zechariah 4:6–10

Zechariah's vision of the horns
Zechariah 1:18–21

His vision of the measuring line
Zechariah 2:1–13

His vision of the High Priest
Zechariah 3:1–10

His vision of the golden candlestick
Zechariah 4:1–5, 11–14

His vision of the flying scroll
Zechariah 5:1–4

His vision of the woman in the basket
Zechariah 5:5–11

For Thought and **Contemplation**

Although the phrase, "Thus saith the Lord", is found 1,904 times in the Old Testament, Zechariah uses it, or its equivalent, close on 90 times. How sad that so many modern pulpits lack this kind of authority. Pray today that God will restore the Old Testament note of authority to the present-day Church.

"When Jesus had finished saying these things, the crowds were amazed at his teaching, because he taught as one who had authority, and not as their teachers of the law." (Matt. 7:28–29)

pointing to Jesus, the coming Messiah: the 'Branch' (3:8), the King Priest (6:13), the humble King, mounted on a donkey (9:9–10), the good shepherd who is sold for thirty pieces of silver (11:4–13) and the one who is pierced (12:10).

Teaching

Haggai aimed to galvanise the Jews into action and complete rebuilding the temple. Zechariah also reminds the Jews to finish this task and spells out the necessity for God's people to be pure. Zechariah concludes with a vision about the coming Messiah.

A Verse to Remember

"On that day ... I will take you, my servant Zerubbabel ... and I will make you like my signet ring, for I have chosen you ..." (Hag. 2:23).

DAY **259**

The decree discovered

Zechariah 6:9–15

**[9]The word of the Lord came to
me: [10]"Take [silver and gold] from
the exiles Heldai, Tobijah and
Jedaiah, who have arrived from
Babylon. Go the same day to the
house of Josiah son of Zephaniah.
[11]Take the silver and gold and
make a crown, and set it on the
head of the high priest, Joshua
son of Jehozadak. [12]Tell him this
is what the Lord Almighty says:
'Here is the man whose name is
the Branch, and he will branch
out from his place and build the
temple of the Lord. [13]It is he who
will build the temple of the Lord,
and he will be clothed with
majesty and will sit and rule on
his throne. And he will be a priest
on his throne. And there will be
harmony between the two.' [14]The
crown will be given to Heldai,
Tobijah, Jedaiah and Hen son of
Zephaniah as a memorial in the
temple of the Lord. [15]Those who
are far away will come and help
to build the temple of the Lord,
and you will know that the Lord
Almighty has sent me to you. This
will happen if you diligently obey
the Lord your God."**

For Thought and **Contemplation**

An effective father, it has been said, needs two outstanding qualifications: firmness in discipline and a readiness to encourage. Some think God has just one of these characteristics – firmness in discipline – but look again at Zech. 8:15 and remind yourself that God is a Father who not only disciplines, but encourages and cares.

"As a father has compassion on his children, so the Lord has compassion on those who fear him ... from everlasting to everlasting the Lord's love is with those who fear him, and his righteousness with their children's children." (Psa. 103:13 & 17)

700 BC | *Assyrians besiege Jerusalem*

Nahum Zephaniah Josiah Nebuchadnezzar

600 BC | Daniel taken to Babylon

Jeremiah Habakkuk

Jerusalem destroyed

FALL OF JUDAH

Ezekiel Exile in Babylon

The completion of the Temple

DAY **260**

Zechariah 9:9–13

9Rejoice greatly, O Daughter
of Zion!
Shout, Daughter of Jerusalem!
See, your king comes to you,
righteous and having salvation,
gentle and riding on a donkey,
on a colt, the foal of a donkey.
10I will take away the chariots
from Ephraim
and the war-horses from
Jerusalem,
and the battle-bow will be
broken.
He will proclaim peace to the
nations.
His rule will extend from sea
to sea
and from the River to the ends
of the earth.
11As for you, because of the blood
of my covenant with you,
I will free your prisoners from the
waterless pit.
12Return to your fortress,
O prisoners of hope;
even now I announce that I will
restore twice as much to you.
13I will bend Judah as I bend
my bow
and fill it with Ephraim. ...

The Lord promises to restore Israel
Zechariah 8:16–23

Temple completed 516 BC

The Temple is completed
Ezra 6:15

Dedication of the Temple
Ezra 6:16–18

The Passover celebration
Ezra 6:19–22

The Restoration 516–400 BC

In praise of God the Saviour
Psalm 146:1–10

In praise of the Lord
Psalm 111:1–10

The happiness of a good person
Psalm 112:1–10

In praise of the Lord's goodness
Psalm 113:1–9

A man saved from death praises God
Psalm 116:1–19

In praise of the Lord
Psalm 117:1–2

Judgment on neighbouring cities
Zechariah 9:1–8

A divine deliverer
Zechariah 9:9–17

For Thought and **Contemplation**

The Temple project is at last complete – a full twenty-three years after it was begun. God's plans and purposes may be hindered or postponed, but they will ultimately be fulfilled. Has there been a hindering of the divine purpose in your life? Then hold on – the day of its fulfilment will most certainly come.

"Being confident of this, that he who began a good work in you will carry it on to completion until the day of Christ Jesus." (Phil. 1:6)

WEEK 38

Zerubbabel and main party return | 500 BC | *Iron Age begins in Britain* | Ezra returns | Malachi | 400 BC

Cyrus | Zechariah | Haggai | 2nd Temple built | Nehemiah rebuilds walls of Jerusalem

Israel's deliverance

The Lord promises deliverance
Zechariah 10:1–12

Destruction to come
Zechariah 11:1–3

The two shepherds
Zechariah 11:4–17

Punishment of Israel's enemies
Zechariah 12:1–9

Israel's repentance and sorrow
Zechariah 12:10–14

Israel's cleansing
Zechariah 13:1–6

The command to kill God's shepherd
Zechariah 13:7–9

Jerusalem and the nations
Zechariah 14:1–15

Israel's restoration
Zechariah 14:16–21

Zechariah 12:10–14

**10"And I will pour out on the house
of David and the inhabitants of
Jerusalem a spirit of grace and
supplication. They will look on me,
the one they have pierced, and
they will mourn for him as one
mourns for an only child, and
grieve bitterly for him as one
grieves for a firstborn son. 11On
that day the weeping in Jerusalem
will be great, like the weeping of
Hadad Rimmon in the plain of
Megiddo. 12The land will mourn,
each clan by itself, with their wives
by themselves: the clan of the
house of David and their wives,
the clan of the house of Nathan
and their wives, 13the clan of the
house of Levi and their wives, the
clan of Shimei and their wives,
14and all the rest of the clans
and their wives.**

For Thought and **Contemplation**

Men have predicted that history will reach its climax through a nuclear holocaust. God has determined that it will reach its climax at the return of His Son. Whom do you believe – men or God? Keep Zechariah 14:1–9 before you, and it will hold you fast in the midst of the greatest threat of world destruction.

"For the Lord himself will come down from heaven, with a loud command, with the voice of the archangel and with the trumpet call of God, and the dead in Christ will rise first. After that, we who are still alive and are left will be caught up together with them in the clouds to meet the Lord in the air ..." (1 Thess. 4:16–17)

a bird's eye view of **Esther**

Place in the Bible	Main Characters	Special Features
Seventeenth Old Testament book; twelfth book of history.	King Xerxes, Queen Vashti, Esther, Mordecai, Haman.	There is no mention of God anywhere in this book, but from beginning to end God's hand is seen in action.

A beauty contest

Esther 3:1–6

**1After these events, King Xerxes
honoured Haman son of
Hammedatha, the Agagite, elevat-
ing him and giving him a seat of
honour higher than that of all the
other nobles. 2All the royal officials
at the king's gate knelt down and
paid honour to Haman, for the king
had commanded this concerning
him. But Mordecai would not kneel
down or pay him honour.
3Then the royal officials at the
king's gate asked Mordecai, "Why
do you disobey the king's com-
mand?" 4Day after day they spoke
to him but he refused to comply.
Therefore they told Haman about
it to see whether Mordecai's
behaviour would be tolerated, for
he had told them he was a Jew.
5When Haman saw that Mordecai
would not kneel down or pay him
honour, he was enraged. 6Yet
having learned who Mordecai's
people were, he scorned the idea
of killing only Mordecai. Instead
Haman looked for a way to
destroy all Mordecai's people,
the Jews, throughout the whole
kingdom of Xerxes.**

Xerxes' feast
Esther 1:1–8

Vashti's rebellion
Esther 1:9–12

Her dethronement
Esther 1:13–22

New queen sought
Esther 2:1–4

Esther brought to Shushan
Esther 2:5, 7–11

Esther made queen
Esther 2:12–17

Feast in honour of Esther
Esther 2:18–20

Mordecai saves the king's life
Esther 2:21–23

Haman's plot
Esther 3:1–7

Haman gains the king's support
Esther 3:8–11

For Thought and **Contemplation**

Esther won the first-ever "Miss World" beauty contest hands down. Yet her real beauty lay, not in her appearance, but in her character. Men judge the outward appearance, but God judges the heart (1 Sam. 16:7).

"Your beauty should not come from outward adornment ... Instead, it should be that of your inner self, the unfading beauty of a gentle and quiet spirit, which is of great worth in God's sight." (1 Pet. 3:3–4)

Jesus and the Book

Esther knew that she was risking her life. Jesus voluntarily gave up his life to rescue us from the stranglehold of sin, as John chapter 10:15 says: "... I lay down my life for the sheep."

Teaching

This book explains the origin of the Jewish Feast of Purim and how, had it not been for Mordecai's astuteness and Esther's courage, the Jews would have been slaughtered. The Jews believed that God was their deliverer.

A Verse to Remember

"'If you remain silent at this time, relief and deliverance for the Jews will arise from another place, but you and your father's family will perish. And who knows but that you have come to royal position for such a time as this?'" (Esth. 4:14).

Building for God

"So the wall was completed ... with the help of our God." (Neh. 6:15,16)
In December 446 BC, Nehemiah learns from his brother Hanani of the pitiful state of Jerusalem. Broken-hearted, Nehemiah begins a time of confession and intercession to God on His people's behalf (1:6–11).

Nehemiah returns to Judah and despite intimidation his confidence in the Lord never wavers. In 53 days the walls are finished. The returning Jewish exiles make a binding covenant to dedicate themselves and the city to the Lord.

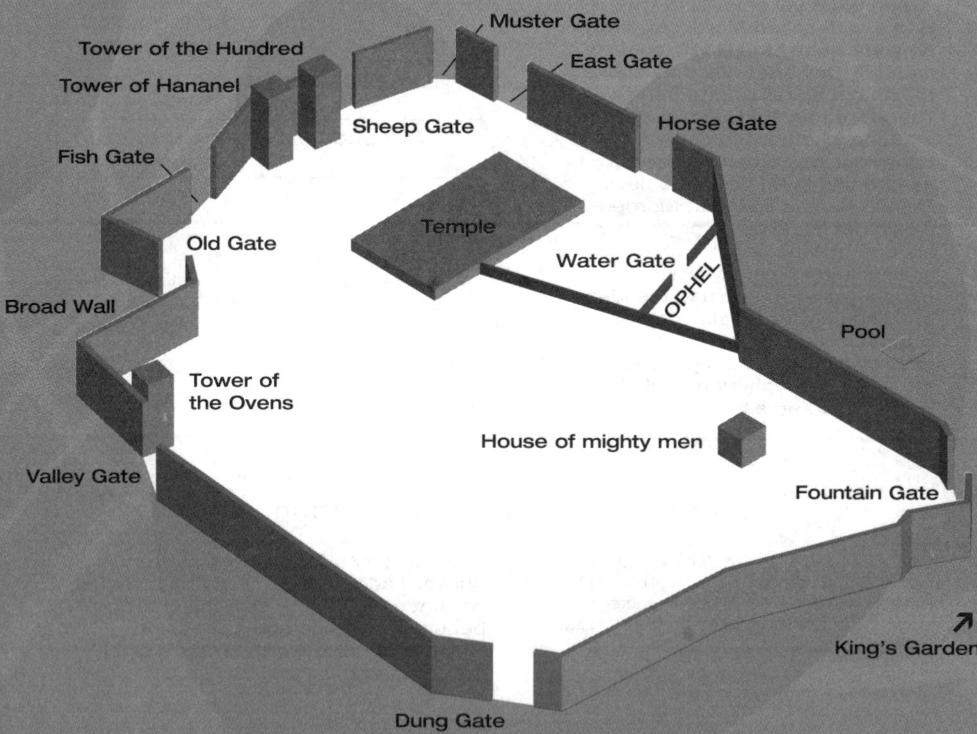

Place names according to RSV, other translations may differ.

The tables are turned

Esther 4:12–17

**12 When Esther's words were
reported to Mordecai, 13 he sent
back this answer: "Do not think
that because you are in the king's
house you alone of all the Jews
will escape. 14 For if you remain
silent at this time, relief and
deliverance for the Jews will arise
from another place, but you and
your father's family will perish.
And who knows but that you have
come to royal position for such
a time as this?"**
**15 Then Esther sent this reply to
Mordecai: 16 "Go, gather together
all the Jews who are in Susa, and
fast for me. Do not eat or drink for
three days, night or day. I and my
maids will fast as you do. When
this is done, I will go to the king,
even though it is against the law.
And if I perish, I perish."**
**17 So Mordecai went away and car-
ried out all of Esther's instructions.**

The command to annihilate all Jews
Esther 3:12–15

Mordecai enlists Esther's help
Esther 4:1–17

Esther's invitation
Esther 5:1–8

Haman's rage against Mordecai
Esther 5:9–14

The king's sleepless night
Esther 6:1–3

Mordecai honoured
Esther 6:4–14

Haman accused
Esther 7:1–6

Haman hanged
Esther 7:7–10

For Thought and **Contemplation**

Do you believe in prayer? *Really* believe? Esther believed in prayer enough to go to the king at an unappointed time with an unlikely request. Underline Esther 5:1–8 in your Bible as a constant reminder that faith sees the invisible, believes the incredible and receives the impossible.

"Ask and it will be given to you; seek and you will find; knock and the door will be opened to you. For everyone who asks receives; he who seeks finds; and to him who knocks, the door will be opened." (Matt. 7:7–8)

WEEK 38

Zerubbabel and main party return | *Iron Age begins in Britain* | Ezra returns | Malachi

500 BC | 400 BC

Cyrus | Zechariah Haggai | 2nd Temple built | Nehemiah rebuilds walls of Jerusalem

The king's edict
Esther 8:1–14

The Jews rejoice
Esther 8:15–17

Their revenge and triumph
Esther 9:1–15

Days of rejoicing
Esther 9:16–19

The Feast of Purim
Esther 9:20–27

Its perpetual celebration
Esther 9:28–32

Mordecai's promotion
Esther 10:1–3

Ezra's commission
Ezra 7:11–20

Esther 10:1–3

1King Xerxes imposed tribute throughout the empire, to its distant shores. 2And all his acts of power and might, together with a full account of the greatness of Mordecai to which the king had raised him, are they not written in the book of the annals of the kings of Media and Persia? 3Mordecai the Jew was second in rank to King Xerxes, pre-eminent among the Jews, and held in high esteem by his many fellow Jews, because he worked for the good of his people and spoke up for the welfare of all the Jews.

For Thought and **Contemplation**

When you are next tempted to think that God is not working because He does not show Himself to you, read again the story of Esther and realise that He is a God who often works behind the scenes. After all, as this book so wonderfully shows, history is really His-story.

"Though the fig-tree does not bud and there are no grapes on the vines, though the olive crop fails and the fields produce no food, though there are no sheep in the pen and no cattle in the stalls, yet I will rejoice in the Lord, I will be joyful in God my Saviour." (Habakkuk 3:17–18)

700 BC *Assyrians besiege Jerusalem* Nahum Zephaniah Josiah Nebuchadnezzar 600 BC Daniel taken to Babylon Jeremiah Habakkuk Jerusalem destroyed FALL OF JUDAH Ezekiel Exile in Babylon

The return to Jerusalem

DAY **265**

Ezra 7:6–10

**6... this Ezra came up from
Babylon. He was a teacher well
versed in the Law of Moses, which
the Lord, the God of Israel, had
given. The king had granted him
everything he asked, for the hand
of the Lord his God was on him.
7Some of the Israelites, including
priests, Levites, singers, gate-
keepers and temple servants, also
came up to Jerusalem in the sev-
enth year of King Artaxerxes.
8Ezra arrived in Jerusalem in the
fifth month of the seventh year of
the king. 9He had begun his jour-
ney from Babylon on the first day
of the first month, and he arrived
in Jerusalem on the first day of the
fifth month, for the gracious hand
of his God was on him. 10For Ezra
had devoted himself to the study
and observance of the Law of the
Lord, and to teaching its decrees
and laws in Israel.**

Artaxerxes' decree
Ezra 7:21–26

Ezra's thanksgiving
Ezra 7:27–28

The exiles who returned with Ezra
Ezra 8:1–14

Ezra returns to Jerusalem 458 BC

The camp site
Ezra 7:9, 8:15

Ezra finds Levites
Ezra 8:16–20

Prayer and fasting
Ezra 8:21–23

The Temple treasures
Ezra 8:24–30

Journey begins
Ezra 8:31

Ezra's arrival at Jerusalem
Ezra 7:6–8, 10, 8:32–36

Ezra's grief
Ezra 9:1–4

His prayer
Ezra 9:5–15

For Thought and **Contemplation**

The secret of Ezra's successful ministry is found in Ezra 7:10. He not only knew what he had to do, but he also did it. As someone has said, "It is of no benefit to know more, unless you first do something with what you know already."

"What good is it, my brothers, if a man claims to have faith but has no deeds? Can such faith save him? ... In the same way, faith by itself, if it is not accompanied by action, is dead." (Jas. 2:14 & 17)

WEEK 38

Zerubbabel and main party return — *Iron Age begins in Britain* — Ezra returns — Malachi

500 BC — 400 BC

Cyrus — Zechariah — Haggai — 2nd Temple built — Nehemiah rebuilds walls of Jerusalem

Ezra plans national gathering
Ezra 10:1–8

He preaches and the people repent
Ezra 10:9–15

Foreign wives divorced
Ezra 10:16–44

Nehemiah's grief
Nehemiah 1:1–4

His prayer
Nehemiah 1:5–11

Nehemiah goes to Jerusalem 437 BC

His request
Nehemiah 2:1–6

Nehemiah appointed governor
Nehemiah 5:14

Letters and escort provided
Nehemiah 2:7–9

Sanballat and Tobiah's indignation
Nehemiah 2:10

Nehemiah's arrival in Jerusalem
Nehemiah 2:11–16

Nehemiah 1:5–10

5 Then I said:
"O Lord, God of heaven, the great
and awesome God, who keeps his
covenant of love with those who
love him and obey his commands,
6 let your ear be attentive and your
eyes open to hear the prayer your
servant is praying before you day
and night for your servants, the
people of Israel. I confess the sins
we Israelites, including myself and
my father's house, have committed
against you. 7 We have acted very
wickedly towards you. We have
not obeyed the commands,
decrees and laws you gave your
servant Moses.
8 Remember the instruction you
gave your servant Moses, saying,
'If you are unfaithful, I will scatter
you among the nations, 9 but if
you return to me and obey my
commands, then even if your
exiled people are at the farthest
horizon, I will gather them from
there and bring them to the place
I have chosen as a dwelling for
my Name.'
10 They are your servants and your
people, whom you redeemed by
your great strength and your
mighty hand."

For Thought and **Contemplation**

Although the centre of Israel's prayer life, the Temple, was established, there was still a need to build the walls. Prayer is important, but so is work. As someone once put it: "We must pray as if it all depended on God, and work as though it all depended on us."

"Therefore, my dear friends, as you have always obeyed – not only in my presence, but now much more in my absence – continue to work out your salvation with fear and trembling, for it is God who works in you to will and to act according to his good purpose." (Phil. 2:12–13)

Nahum Zephaniah Josiah Nebuchadnezzar Jerusalem destroyed
700 BC | 600 BC | FALL OF JUDAH
Assyrians besiege Jerusalem Daniel taken to Babylon Ezekiel
Jeremiah Habakkuk Exile in Babylon

Rebuilding the walls

DAY **267**

Nehemiah 4:1–6

**1When Sanballat heard that we
were rebuilding the wall, he
became angry and was greatly
incensed. He ridiculed the Jews,
2and in the presence of his associ-
ates and the army of Samaria, he
said, "What are those feeble Jews
doing? Will they restore their wall?
Will they offer sacrifices? Will they
finish in a day? Can they bring the
stones back to life from those
heaps of rubble – burned as
they are?"
3Tobiah the Ammonite, who was
at his side, said, "What they are
building – if even a fox climbed up
on it, he would break down their
wall of stones!"
4Hear us, O our God, for we are
despised. Turn their insults back
on their own heads. Give them over
as plunder in a land of captivity.
5Do not cover up their guilt or blot
out their sins from your sight, for
they have thrown insults in the
face of the builders.
6So we rebuilt the wall till all of it
reached half its height, for the
people worked with all their heart.**

Nehemiah's encouragement to rebuild
Nehemiah 2:17–18

The contempt of Sanballat and others
Nehemiah 2:19–20

List of builders
Nehemiah 3:1–16

The Levites
Nehemiah 3:17–21

The priests
Nehemiah 3:22–26

Other builders
Nehemiah 3:27–32

Nehemiah overcomes ridicule
Nehemiah 4:1–6

The conspiracy
Nehemiah 4:7–15

Nehemiah's precautions
Nehemiah 4:16–23

The people's complaint
Nehemiah 5:1–5

Nehemiah's rebuke
Nehemiah 5:6–11

The restitution
Nehemiah 5:12–13

For Thought and **Contemplation**

One of the characteristics of God's people, in the New Testament as well as the Old, is that sometimes, instead of fighting the enemy, they turn to fighting each other. How Satan must enjoy these lapses! Pray that Christians might come to see the stupidity of this.

"How good and pleasant it is when brothers live together in unity! ... It is as if the dew of Hermon were falling on Mount Zion. For there the Lord bestows his blessing, even life for evermore." (Psa. 133: 1 & 3)

WEEK 39

Zerubbabel and main party return | *Iron Age begins in Britain* | Ezra returns | Malachi

500 BC | 400 BC

Cyrus | Zechariah Haggai | 2nd Temple built | Nehemiah rebuilds walls of Jerusalem

DAY 268 Rebuilding programme completed

Nehemiah's unselfishness
Nehemiah 5:15–19

Plots against Nehemiah
Nehemiah 6:1–14

Rebuilding completed
Nehemiah 6:15–19

Hanani and Hananiah to protect Jerusalem
Nehemiah 7:1–3

The first return
1 Chronicles 9:2–9

The priests
1 Chronicles 9:10–13

The Levites
1 Chronicles 9:14–16

The gatekeepers
1 Chronicles 9:17–27

Other tasks of the Levites
1 Chronicles 9:28–34

The inhabitants of Jerusalem
Nehemiah 11:1–9

Nehemiah 7:1–3

1After the wall had been rebuilt and
I had set the doors in place, the
gatekeepers and the singers and
the Levites were appointed. 2I put
in charge of Jerusalem my brother
Hanani, along with Hananiah the
commander of the citadel,
because he was a man of integrity
and feared God more than most
men do. 3I said to them, "The
gates of Jerusalem are not to be
opened until the sun is hot. While
the gatekeepers are still on duty,
have them shut the doors and bar
them. Also appoint residents of
Jerusalem as guards, some at
their posts and some near their
own houses."

For Thought and **Contemplation**

Ever heard of the "Nehemiah Management Principles"? Then read this book carefully, and you will see how expertly he got God's task done, *through people*. Good supervision, it has been said, is "the art of getting ordinary people to do extraordinary work." Is God saying something to you in all this?

"Just as each of us has one body with many members, and these members do not all have the same function, so in Christ we who are many form one body, and each member belongs to all the others. We have different gifts, according to the grace given us. ..." (Rom. 12:4–6)

Zerubbabel and main party return
500 BC
Iron Age begins in Britain
Ezra returns
Malachi
400 BC
Cyrus
Zechariah Haggai
2nd Temple built
Nehemiah rebuilds walls of Jerusalem

Restoration of Israel

Rebuilt walls
Nehemiah Ch. 1–7

- plans received
- building commences
- work is completed

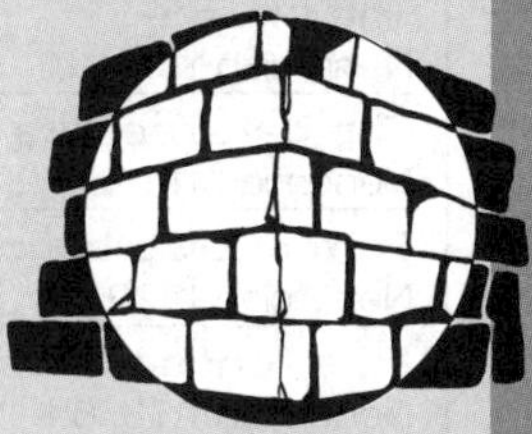

Renewed worship
Neh. Ch. 8–10

- the law is read
- repentance follows
- a celebration of worship

Restored nation
Neh. Ch. 11–13

- people placed in cities
- walls are dedicated
- Temple is cleansed

about 25 years' duration

DAY **269** The Law is read

The priests
Nehemiah 11:10–14

The Levites
Nehemiah 11:15–18

The gatekeepers
Nehemiah 11:19

Further distribution of the people
Nehemiah 11:20–36

Ezra reads the Law
Nehemiah 7:73, 8:1–12

Feast of Tabernacles
Nehemiah 8:13–18

The people confess their sins
Nehemiah 9:1–4

God's goodness remembered
Nehemiah 9:5–31

Nehemiah 8:1–6

**1... all the people assembled as
one man in the square before the
Water Gate. They told Ezra the
scribe to bring out the Book of the
Law of Moses, which the Lord had
commanded for Israel.
2So on the first day of the seventh
month, Ezra the priest brought the
Law before the assembly, which
was made up of men and women
and all who were able to under-
stand. 3He read it aloud from
daybreak till noon as he faced the
square before the Water Gate in
the presence of the men, women
and others who could understand.
And all the people listened
attentively to the Book of the Law.
4Ezra the scribe stood on a high
wooden platform built for the
occasion. Beside him on his right
stood Mattithiah, Shema, Anaiah,
Uriah, Hilkiah and Maaseiah; and
on his left were Pedaiah, Mishael,
Malkijah, Hashum, Hashbaddanah,
Zechariah and Meshullam.
5Ezra opened the book. All the
people could see him because he
was standing above them; and as
he opened it, the people all stood
up. 6Ezra praised the Lord, the
great God ...**

For Thought and **Contemplation**

One of the great principles of Old Testament worship was the way in which they reminded themselves of God's goodness to them in the past. Take a lesson from their example today. Recite at least ten instances of how God has blessed your life in the past year.

"Yet this I call to mind and therefore I have hope: Because of the Lord's great love we are not consumed, for his compassions never fail." (Lamentations 3:21–22)

700 BC
Assyrians besiege Jerusalem
Nahum Zephaniah Josiah Nebuchadnezzar
600 BC
Daniel taken to Babylon
Jeremiah Habakkuk
Jerusalem destroyed
FALL OF JUDAH
Ezekiel
Exile in Babylon

Nehemiah 9:32–37

**[32]"Now therefore, O our God, the
great, mighty and awesome God,
who keeps his covenant of love,
do not let all this hardship seem
trifling in your eyes – the hardship
that has come upon us, upon our
kings and leaders, upon our
priests and prophets, upon our
fathers and all your people, from
the days of the kings of Assyria
until today. [33]In all that has hap-
pened to us, you have been just;
you have acted faithfully, while we
did wrong. [34]Our kings, our leaders,
our priests and our fathers did not
follow your law; they did not pay
attention to your commands or the
warnings you gave them. [35]Even
while they were in their kingdom,
enjoying your great goodness to
them in the spacious and fertile
land you gave them, they did not
serve you or turn from their
evil ways.**

**[36]"But see, we are slaves today,
slaves in the land you gave our
forefathers so that they could eat
its fruit and the other good things
it produces. [37]Because of our sins,
its abundant harvest goes to the
kings you have placed over us. ..."**

God's goodness and mercy remembered
Nehemiah 9:32–37

Covenant made
Nehemiah 9:38

The people sign the covenant
Nehemiah 10:1–27

The covenant
Nehemiah 10:28–39

The dedication of the wall
Nehemiah 12:27–43

In praise of God the Almighty
Psalm 147:1–20

For Thought and **Contemplation**

In light of what you have read today, this would be an excellent time to renew any promises or vows you have made to the Lord. Are you married? Then spend some quiet moments re-affirming your commitment. Are you single? The commit yourself to serving Him with undivided attention (1 Cor. 7:32–34).

"May the God of peace, who through the blood of the eternal covenant brought back from the dead our Lord Jesus, that great Shepherd of the sheep, equip you with everything good for doing his will, and may he work in us what is pleasing to him, through Jesus Christ, to whom be glory for ever and ever. Amen." (Heb. 13:20–21)

WEEK 39

Zerubbabel and main party return | *Iron Age begins in Britain* | Ezra returns | Malachi

500 BC | 400 BC

Cyrus | Zechariah Haggai | 2nd Temple built | Nehemiah rebuilds walls of Jerusalem

DAY 271 The law of the Lord

A call to praise God
Psalm 148:1–14

Hymns of praise
Psalm 149:1–9, 150:1–6

Tobiah expelled from the Temple
Nehemiah 13:4–9

Temple order restored
Nehemiah 12:44–47

Separation from foreigners
Nehemiah 13:1–3

The law of the Lord
Psalm 119:1–8

Obedience to it
Psalm 119:9–24

Determination to obey
Psalm 119:25–32

A prayer for understanding
Psalm 119:33–40

Trusting God's law
Psalm 119:41–56

Devotion to it
Psalm 119:57–64

The value and justice of it
Psalm 119:65–80

Nehemiah 13:4–9

**4 Before this, Eliashib the priest had been put in charge of the storerooms of the house of our God. He was closely associated with Tobiah,
5 and he had provided him with a large room formerly used to store the grain offerings and incense and temple articles, and also the tithes of grain, new wine and oil prescribed for the Levites, singers and gatekeepers, as well as the contributions for the priests.
6 But while all this was going on, I was not in Jerusalem, for in the thirty-second year of Artaxerxes king of Babylon I had returned to the king. Some time later I asked his permission
7 and came back to Jerusalem. Here I learned about the evil thing Eliashib had done in providing Tobiah a room in the courts of the house of God.
8 I was greatly displeased and threw all Tobiah's household goods out of the room.
9 I gave orders to purify the rooms, and then I put back into them the equipment of the house of God, with the grain offerings and the incense.**

For Thought and **Contemplation**

Revival could not come to Israel while Tobiah was living in the Temple. A Tobiah in God's House is like having the devil in the church vestry. Would to God we had men in the Church today who would follow Nehemiah's example, and expel from the midst of God's people all those things which are not of Him.

"Jesus ... overturned the tables of the money changers and the benches of those selling doves. 'It is written,' he said to them, '"My house will be called a house of prayer," but you are making it a "den of robbers".' " (Matt. 21:12–13)

a bird's eye view of **Psalms**

Place in the Bible

Nineteenth Old Testament book; second book of poetry and wisdom.

Special Features

Israel's hymn book brings together a wide variety of hymns, some praising God, others lamenting national sin, some written for public worship and others for private prayer.

Nehemiah's final reforms

Nehemiah 13:10–14

[10]I also learned that the portions
assigned to the Levites had not
been given to them, and that all
the Levites and singers responsible
for the service had gone back to
their own fields. [11]So I rebuked the
officials and asked them, "Why is
the house of God neglected?"
Then I called them together and
stationed them at their posts.
[12]All Judah brought the tithes of
grain, new wine and oil into the
storerooms. [13]I put Shelemiah the
priest, Zadok the scribe, and a
Levite named Pedaiah in charge
of the storerooms and made
Hanan son of Zaccur, the son
of Mattaniah, their assistant,
because these men were
considered trustworthy. They were
made responsible for distributing
the supplies to their brothers.
[14]Remember me for this, O my
God, and do not blot out what
I have so faithfully done for the
house of my God and its services.

Prayer for deliverance
Psalm 119:81–88

Faith in God's law
Psalm 119:89–96

Love for it
Psalm 119:97–112

Safety in it
Psalm 119:113–128

Desire to obey it
Psalm 119:129–136

Its justice
Psalm 119:137–144

A plea for help
Psalm 119:145–176

True happiness
Psalm 1:1–6

Tithing and worship re-established
Nehemiah 13:10–14

Sabbath keeping violated
Nehemiah 13:15–22

For Thought and **Contemplation**

One of Nehemiah's great reforms was to re-establish the principle of tithing for the support of the priests. The work of God was neglected because the workmen were not properly rewarded. Could this be a reform that is needed in your church? If so, then ask the Lord just what He would have you do about it.

"Each man should give what he has decided in his heart to give, not reluctantly or under compulsion, for God loves a cheerful giver." (2 Cor. 9:7)

Jesus and the Book

Many Psalms which apparently refer to David can be seen to be further fulfilled in Jesus, the Messiah.

Teaching

The Psalms present God as creator, deliverer, protector, forgiver, provider, guide, the One worthy of praise, thanksgiving and worship.

A Verse to Remember

"The Lord is my rock, my fortress and my deliverer; my God is my rock, in whom I take refuge" (Psalm 18:2).

Malachi's prophecy

Intermarriage rebuked
Nehemiah 13:23–29

Priesthood cleansed
Nehemiah 13:30–31

The Lord's love for Israel
Malachi 1:1–5

The Lord reprimands the priests
Malachi 1:6–14, 2:1–9

The people's unfaithfulness
Malachi 2:10–16

The Lord will judge His people
Malachi 2:17, 3:1–5

The payment of tithes
Malachi 3:6–12

God's promise of mercy
Malachi 3:13–18

Greece the world power 333–63 BC

Coming Day of the Lord
Malachi 4:1–6

Malachi 4:1–6

**1"Surely the day is coming; it
will burn like a furnace. All the
arrogant and every evildoer will
be stubble, and that day that is
coming will set them on fire," says
the Lord Almighty. "Not a root or a
branch will be left to them. 2But for
you who revere my name, the sun
of righteousness will rise with
healing in its wings. And you will
go out and leap like calves
released from the stall. 3Then you
will trample down the wicked; they
will be ashes under the soles of
your feet on the day when I do
these things," says the Lord
Almighty.
4"Remember the law of my servant
Moses, the decrees and laws I
gave him at Horeb for all Israel.
5"See, I will send you the prophet
Elijah before that great and
dreadful day of the Lord comes.
6He will turn the hearts of the
fathers to their children, and the
hearts of the children to their
fathers; or else I will come and
strike the land with a curse."**

For Thought and **Contemplation**

The last word of the Old Testament is the "promise of a curse" that would come upon an unfaithful and disobedient people. How different from the last chapters of the New Testament which show all sin removed from the universe and promise eternal joy and everlasting peace.

"Christ redeemed us from the curse of the law by becoming a curse for us, for it is written: 'Cursed is everyone who is hung on a tree.' He redeemed us in order that the blessing given to Abraham might come to the Gentiles through Christ Jesus ..." (Gal. 3:13–14)

a bird's eye view of **Malachi**

Place in the Bible

Thirty-ninth Old Testament book; seventeenth book of prophecy.

Two announcements

Luke 1:1–4

[1]Many have undertaken to draw up an account of the things that have been fulfilled among us, [2]just as they were handed down to us by those who from the first were eye-witnesses and servants of the word. [3]Therefore, since I myself have carefully investigated everything from the beginning, it seemed good also to me to write an orderly account for you, most excellent Theophilus, [4]so that you may know the certainty of the things you have been taught.

Prefaces to Synoptic Gospels
Matthew 1:1, Mark 1:1, Luke 1:1–4

Preface to John's Gospel
John 1:1–5

Rome the World Power 63 BC–AD 476

Two genealogies of Jesus Christ
Matthew 1:2–17, Luke 3:23–38

Birth of John the Baptist announced
Luke 1:5–25

Birth of Jesus Christ announced
Luke 1:26–38

For Thought and **Contemplation**

Many Christians skip over the genealogy of Christ because they find it dull and uninteresting. But how wonderfully it underlines the truth that, when Christ came to save, He did not just come *near* to the human race, He came *into* it. The Son of God became the Son of Man, that the sons of men might become the sons of God.

"For to us a child is born, to us a son is given, and the government will be on his shoulders. And he will be called Wonderful Counsellor, Mighty God, Everlasting Father, Prince of Peace." (Isa. 9:6)

Jesus and the Book

Malachi predicts that the prophet Elijah would come before the Messiah, and Jesus identified John the Baptist as this person (Matt. 11:10–11).

Teaching

Hard hearts, abuse of the poor and needy, idolatry and covetousness are the order of the day. God's people need a Deliverer from God's judgment.

A Verse to Remember

"Bring the whole tithe into the storehouse, that there may be food in my house ... and see if I will not throw open the floodgates of heaven and pour out so much blessing that you will not have room enough for it" (Mal. 3:10).

Section 9

Once again, congratulations. You have now read three-quarters of the Bible and built a solid foundation of truth on which the New Testament can rest. At CWR there are people praying for you to finish the course so even if you are a little behind take comfort from what you have already achieved and press on to reach the goal.

10

In this section

The birth and childhood of Jesus
John the Baptist's message
Jesus' call of His disciples
His teaching and healing ministry
The triumphal entry into Jerusalem

The birth of Jesus Christ

Elizabeth's greeting to Mary
Luke 1:39–45

Mary praised God
Luke 1:46–55

The birth of John the Baptist 6 BC

Mary stays with Elizabeth
Luke 1:56

Birth of John the Baptist
Luke 1:57–66

Zechariah's prophecy
Luke 1:67–79

John's early years
Luke 1:80

The announcement to Joseph
Matthew 1:18–24

Birth of Jesus Christ 5 BC

The birth of Jesus
Luke 2:1–7, Matthew 1:25

The angels and the shepherds
Luke 2:8–20

Circumcision of Jesus
Luke 2:21

Presentation in the Temple
Luke 2:22–38

Matthew 1:18–24

**18 This is how the birth of Jesus
Christ came about: His mother
Mary was pledged to be married
to Joseph, but before they came
together, she was found to be
with child through the Holy Spirit.
19 Because Joseph her husband
was a righteous man and did not
want to expose her to public
disgrace, he had in mind to
divorce her quietly.
20 But after he had considered this,
an angel of the Lord appeared to
him in a dream and said, "Joseph
son of David, do not be afraid to
take Mary home as your wife,
because what is conceived in her
is from the Holy Spirit. 21 She will
give birth to a son, and you are to
give him the name Jesus, because
he will save his people from
their sins."
22 All this took place to fulfil what
the Lord had said through the
prophet: 23 "The virgin will be with
child and will give birth to a son,
and they will call him Immanuel" –
which means, "God with us."
24 When Joseph woke up, he did
what the angel of the Lord had
commanded him and took Mary
home as his wife.**

For Thought and **Contemplation**

How slow and unhurried God must have seemed to those who knew the prophecies concerning Christ's first coming. Yet God is always right on time – never a moment too soon, and never a moment too late. He is a punctual God. Keep this thought in mind the next time you are tempted to think the Almighty's schedules are mistimed.

"But when the time had fully come, God sent his Son, born of a woman, born under law, to redeem those under law, that we might receive the full rights of sons." (Gal. 4:4–5)

a bird's eye view of **Luke**

Place in the Bible	Written by:	Special Features
Third New Testament book, third Gospel.	Luke.	Dr Luke's observant eye lays special emphasis on certain people and things in his Gospel: prayer, joy, the Holy Spirit, the early life of Jesus, children, women and social outcasts.

Jesus' childhood

Luke 2:41–49

**41Every year his parents went
to Jerusalem for the Feast of the
Passover. 42When he was twelve
years old, they went up to the
Feast, according to the custom.
43After the Feast was over, while
his parents were returning home,
the boy Jesus stayed behind in
Jerusalem, but they were unaware
of it. 44Thinking he was in their
company, they travelled on for a
day. Then they began looking for
him among their relatives and
friends. 45When they did not find
him, they went back to Jerusalem
to look for him. 46After three days
they found him in the temple
courts, sitting among the teachers,
listening to them and asking them
questions. 47Everyone who heard
him was amazed at his under-
standing and his answers. 48When
his parents saw him, they were
astonished. His mother said to
him, "Son, why have you treated
us like this? Your father and I have
been anxiously searching for you."
49"Why were you searching for
me?" he asked. "Didn't you know
I had to be in my Father's house?"**

The wise men
Matthew 2:1–12

The flight to Egypt
Matthew 2:13–18

From Egypt to Nazareth
Matthew 2:19–23, Luke 2:39

Jesus' childhood in Nazareth
Luke 2:40

Birth of Paul: AD 10–15 approx.

Jesus in the Temple
Luke 2:41–50

Jesus' early life
Luke 2:51–52

Start of John the Baptist's ministry
Matthew 3:1–6, Mark 1:2–6, Luke 3:1–6, John 1:6–18

For Thought and **Contemplation**

One of the first things children demonstrate when growing up is the truth of the Scripture that says: "Foolishness is bound in the heart of a child" (Prov. 22:15). Foolishness appears in all they say and do. How different with Jesus. His wisdom baffled the sages of His day. And why? Because it was the wisdom of God!

"The Word became flesh and made his dwelling among us. We have seen his glory, the glory of the One and Only, who came from the Father, full of grace and truth." (Jn. 1:14)

Jesus and the Book

Luke presents Jesus Christ as the One who showed compassion to men and women, and who came to seek and to save lost sinners and offer God's priceless gift of salvation.

Teaching

Luke sets down an orderly, meticulous account of the life, death and resurrection of Jesus. His purpose, as stated in 1:3–4, was to strengthen the faith of Gentiles and to show that Jesus Christ is the Saviour of every kind of person in the world.

A Verse to Remember

"'For the Son of Man came to seek and to save what was lost'" (Luke 19:10)

The temptation of Jesus

John the Baptist's ministry begins AD 25

John the Baptist's message
Matthew 3:7–10, Luke 3:7–14

His introduction of Christ
Matthew 3:11–12, Mark 1:7–8, Luke 3:15–18, John 1:19–28

The baptism of Jesus
Matthew 3:13–17, Mark 1:9–11, Luke 3:21–22

John's declaration
John 1:29–34

The temptation in the wilderness
Matthew 4:1–11, Mark 1:12–13, Luke 4:1–13

The first three disciples
John 1:35–42

Philip and Nathanael
John 1:43–51

Luke 4:1–8

**1 Jesus, full of the Holy Spirit,
returned from the Jordan and
was led by the Spirit in the desert,
2 where for forty days he was
tempted by the devil. He ate
nothing during those days, and at
the end of them he was hungry.
3 The devil said to him, "If you are
the Son of God, tell this stone to
become bread."
4 Jesus answered, "It is written:
'Man does not live on bread
alone.'"
5 The devil led him up to a high
place and showed him in an
instant all the kingdoms of the
world. 6 And he said to him, "I will
give you all their authority and
splendour, for it has been given
to me, and I can give it to anyone
I want to. 7 So if you worship me,
it will all be yours."
8 Jesus answered, "It is written:
'Worship the Lord your God and
serve him only.'"**

For Thought and **Contemplation**

What a contrast exists between the temptation of the first Adam and that of Christ, who is called in Scripture the last Adam. The first Adam failed while feasting in a garden, but the second Adam triumphed while fasting in a wilderness. And because He triumphed – so can you!

"So it is written: 'The first man Adam became a living being'; the last Adam, a life-giving spirit. The spiritual did not come first, but the natural, and after that the spiritual. The first man was of the dust of the earth, the second man from heaven." (1 Cor. 15:45–47)

WEEK 40

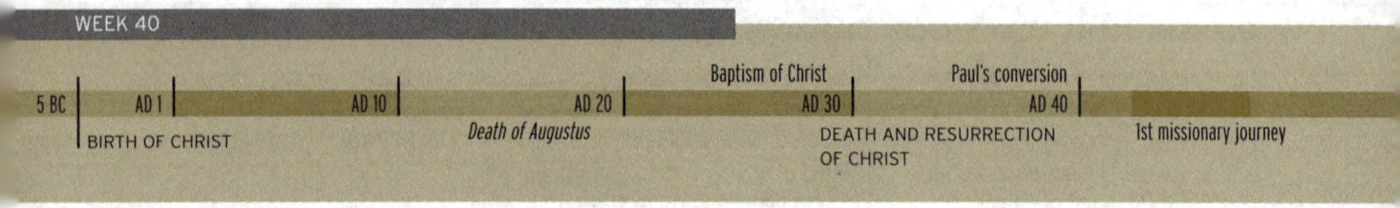

Jesus and John

DAY **278**

John 3:25–30

**25 An argument developed between
some of John's disciples and a
certain Jew over the matter of
ceremonial washing. 26 They came
to John and said to him, "Rabbi,
that man who was with you on the
other side of the Jordan – the one
you testified about – well, he is
baptising, and everyone is going
to him."
27 To this John replied, "A man can
receive only what is given him
from heaven. 28 You yourselves can
testify that I said, 'I am not the
Christ but am sent ahead of him.'
29 The bride belongs to the bride-
groom. The friend who attends
the bridegroom waits and listens
for him, and is full of joy when he
hears the bridegroom's voice.
That joy is mine, and it is now
complete. 30 He must become
greater; I must become less.**

The wedding in Cana
John 2:1–11

Jesus in Capernaum
John 2:12

Jesus in the Temple
John 2:13–22

Jesus' knowledge of human nature
John 2:23–25

Jesus and Nicodemus
John 3:1–21

Jesus and John
John 3:22–24

John's testimony
John 3:25–36

The imprisonment of John
Luke 3:19–20

Jesus leaves Judea
Matthew 4:12, John 4:1–3

Jesus and the woman at the well
John 4:4–26

For Thought and **Contemplation**

John the Baptist faced a dilemma that, sooner or later, comes to every one of us: who is to be first – me, or Jesus? You know how John decided: it would be Jesus! "He must become greater; I must become less." What decision have you reached about this momentous issue?

"I have been crucified with Christ and I no longer live, but Christ lives in me. The life I live in the body, I live by faith in the Son of God, who loved me and gave himself for me." (Gal. 2:20)

AD 50 | AD 60 | Paul in Rome | AD 70 | AD 80 | AD 90 | Revelation | AD 100

2nd missionary journey
3rd missionary journey
Death of Paul
Death of Nero
Destruction of Jerusalem
Completion of Colosseum in Rome
Destruction of Pompeii and Herculaneum
Death of John

Jesus' early ministry

Jesus in Samaria
John 4:27–42

Jesus preaches the Gospel
Matthew 4:17, Mark 1:14–15, Luke 4:14–15, John 4:43–45

Jesus heals an official's son
John 4:46–54

Jesus is rejected at Nazareth
Luke 4:16–30

Jesus leaves Nazareth
Matthew 4:13–16

Jesus calls four fishermen
Matthew 4:18–22, Mark 1:16–20, Luke 5:1–11

Jesus teaches in the synagogue
Mark 1:21–22, Luke 4:31–32

The man with an evil spirit
Mark 1:23–28

Mark 1:21–28

**21They went to Capernaum, and
when the Sabbath came, Jesus
went into the synagogue and
began to teach. 22The people were
amazed at his teaching, because
he taught them as one who had
authority, not as the teachers of
the law. 23Just then a man in their
synagogue who was possessed
by an evil spirit cried out, 24"What
do you want with us, Jesus of
Nazareth? Have you come to
destroy us? I know who you are -
the Holy One of God!"
25"Be quiet!" said Jesus sternly.
"Come out of him!" 26The evil spirit
shook the man violently and came
out of him with a shriek.
27The people were all so amazed
that they asked each other, "What
is this? A new teaching - and with
authority! He even gives orders to
evil spirits and they obey him."
28News about him spread quickly
over the whole region of Galilee.**

For Thought and **Contemplation**

Anyone who embarks upon an effective ministry for God will, at some time or other, experience rejection. Jesus did – and so will you. And how you handle that rejection will determine whether your ministry will go backward or forward. Jesus went forward – and in His strength, so can you.

"For we do not have a high priest who is unable to sympathise with our weaknesses, but we have one who has been tempted in every way, just as we are - yet was without sin." (Heb. 4:15)

WEEK 40

5 BC | AD 1 | AD 10 | AD 20 | AD 30 | AD 40

BIRTH OF CHRIST

Death of Augustus

Baptism of Christ

DEATH AND RESURRECTION OF CHRIST

Paul's conversion

1st missionary journey

The main highlights of Christ's life

1. **His birth** (Lk. 2:1–7)
2. **The adoration by the shepherds** (Lk. 2:8–20)
3. **The dedication in Jerusalem** (Lk. 2:21–38)
4. **The worship by the wise men** (Matt. 2:1–12)
5. **Flight into Egypt** (Matt. 2:13–18)
6. **Temple visit at age twelve** (Lk. 2:41–50)
7. **His baptism** (Matt. 3:13–17)

8. **His temptation** (Matt. 4:1–11)
9. **Introduction by John the Baptist** (Jn. 1:29)
10. **First Temple cleansing** (Jn. 2:13–25)
11. **Teaching about the new birth** (Jn. 3:1–21)
12. **The choice of the twelve** (Matt. 10:1–4)
13. **Imprisonment and execution of John** (Matt. 14:1–12)

14. **Peter's great confession** (Matt. 16:13–20)
15. **The transfiguration** (Matt. 17:1–13)
16. **His triumphal entry** (Matt. 21:1–11)
17. **Weeping over Jerusalem** (Matt. 23:37–39; Lk. 19:41)
18. **In the upper room** (Jn. 13–14)
19. **In Gethsemane** (Jn. 18:1–11)

20. **His arrest and trials** (Jn. 18:12–19:15)
21. **The crucifixion** (Jn. 19:16–24)
22. **The resurrection** (Matt. 28:1–7)
23. **The ten appearances**
24. **The ascension** (Lk. 24:51)

DAY 280 Jesus heals many

The man with an evil spirit
Luke 4:33–37

Jesus heals many people
Matthew 8:14–17, Mark 1:29–34, Luke 4:38–41

Jesus in Galilee
Matthew 4:23–25, Mark 1:35–39, Luke 4:42–44

Jesus heals a leper
Matthew 8:2–4, Mark 1:40–45, Luke 5:12–16

He heals a paralysed man
Matthew 9:1–8, Mark 2:1–12, Luke 5:17–26

Luke 5:12–16

**12 While Jesus was in one of the
towns, a man came along who
was covered with leprosy. When
he saw Jesus, he fell with his face
to the ground and begged him,
"Lord, if you are willing, you can
make me clean."
13 Jesus reached out his hand and
touched the man. "I am willing," he
said. "Be clean!" And immediately
the leprosy left him.
14 Then Jesus ordered him, "Don't
tell anyone, but go, show yourself
to the priest and offer the
sacrifices that Moses commanded
for your cleansing, as a testimony
to them."
15 Yet the news about him spread
all the more, so that crowds of
people came to hear him and to
be healed of their sicknesses.
16 But Jesus often withdrew to lonely
places and prayed.**

For Thought and **Contemplation**

Did the healing ministry of Jesus cease when He left this world and returned to heaven? Many think so. What do *you* believe? If you are unsure about this, turn to Hebrews 13:8 and settle the matter once and for all.

"He himself bore our sins in his body on the tree, so that we might die to sins and live for righteousness; by his wounds you have been healed." (1 Pet. 2:24)

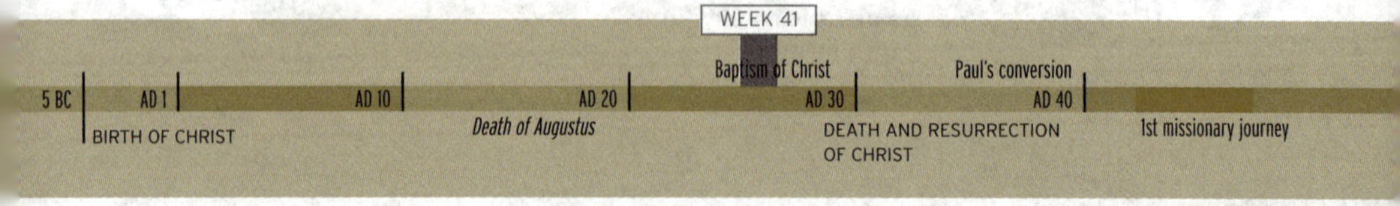

Mark 2:13–17

[13]Once again Jesus went out beside the lake. A large crowd came to him, and he began to teach them. [14]As he walked along, he saw Levi son of Alphaeus sitting at the tax collector's booth. "Follow me," Jesus told him, and Levi got up and followed him.

[15]While Jesus was having dinner at Levi's house, many tax collectors and "sinners" were eating with him and his disciples, for there were many who followed him. [16]When the teachers of the law who were Pharisees saw him eating with the "sinners" and tax collectors, they asked his disciples: "Why does he eat with tax collectors and 'sinners'?"

[17]On hearing this, Jesus said to them, "It is not the healthy who need a doctor, but the sick. I have not come to call the righteous, but sinners."

Jesus calls Matthew
Matthew 9:9–13, Mark 2:13–17, Luke 5:27–32

The question about fasting
Matthew 9:14–17, Mark 2:18–22, Luke 5:33–39

The healing at the pool
John 5:1–9

The Jews' displeasure
John 5:10–18

Jesus' response
John 5:19–23

He speaks of His authority
John 5:24–29

His witnesses
John 5:30–47

For Thought and **Contemplation**

Do you know the difference between "power" and "authority"? Imagine a huge transporter coming down the High Street. That's *power*. Then imagine a policeman stepping out, holding up his hand and commanding the huge vehicle to stop. That's *authority*. And Christ gives that same authority to you and me (see Luke 9:1).

"For by him all things were created: things in heaven and on earth, visible and invisible, whether thrones or powers or rulers or authorities; all things were created by him and for him. He is before all things, and in him all things hold together." (Col. 1:16–17)

AD 50 | AD 60 | AD 70 | AD 80 | AD 90 | AD 100

2nd missionary journey
3rd missionary journey
Paul in Rome
Death of Paul
Death of Nero
Destruction of Jerusalem
Completion of Colosseum in Rome
Destruction of Pompeii and Herculaneum
Revelation
Death of John

Jesus chooses the Twelve

Luke 6:12–16

12 One of those days Jesus went
out to a mountainside to pray, and
spent the night praying to God.
13 When morning came, he called
his disciples to him and chose
twelve of them, whom he also
designated apostles: 14 Simon
(whom he named Peter), his
brother Andrew, James, John,
Philip, Bartholomew, 15 Matthew,
Thomas, James son of Alphaeus,
Simon who was called the Zealot,
16 Judas son of James, and Judas
Iscariot, who became a traitor.

For Thought and **Contemplation**

God calls no one to a special ministry or service for Him without providing the resources by which that ministry can be accomplished. And remember this – no matter the task ahead of you, it is never as great as the power behind you.

"Brothers, think of what you were when you were called. Not many of you were wise by human standards ... But God chose the foolish things of the world to shame the wise; God chose the weak things of the world to shame the strong. He chose the lowly things of this world and the despised things ..." (1 Cor. 1:26–28)

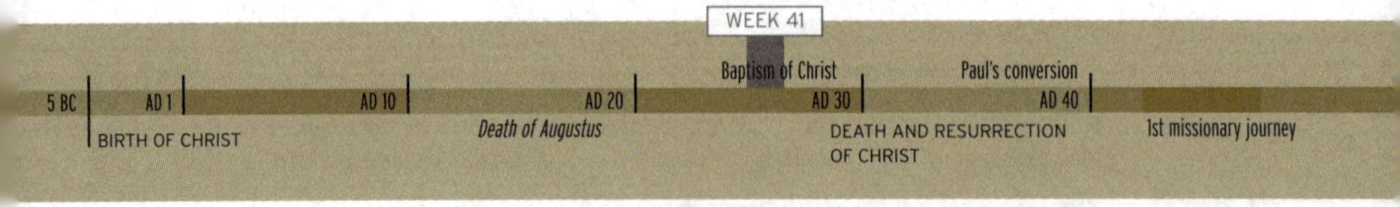

The Sermon on the Mount

Matthew 7:7–12

**[7]“Ask and it will be given to you;
seek and you will find; knock and
the door will be opened to you.
[8]For everyone who asks receives;
he who seeks finds; and to him
who knocks, the door will be
opened.
[9]“Which of you, if his son asks for
bread, will give him a stone? [10]Or
if he asks for a fish, will give him
a snake? [11]If you, then, though you
are evil, know how to give good
gifts to your children, how much
more will your Father in heaven
give good gifts to those who ask
him! [12]So in everything, do to
others what you would have them
do to you, for this sums up the
Law and the Prophets.**

Jesus teaching about anger, adultery and divorce
Matthew 5:21–32

Vows and revenge
Matthew 5:33–42

Love for enemies
Matthew 5:43–48

Teaching about giving
Matthew 6:1–4

Teaching about prayer and fasting
Matthew 6:5–18

Riches in heaven
Matthew 6:19–23

God and possessions
Matthew 6:24–34

Judging others
Matthew 7:1–6

Our heavenly Father
Matthew 7:7–12

Further teaching
Matthew 7:13–23

The wise man and the foolish man
Matthew 7:24–27

Jesus' authority
Matthew 7:28–29

For Thought and **Contemplation**

Some Christians are more concerned about beliefs than behaviour, others about behaviour more than beliefs. The Sermon on the Mount emphasises the necessity of both. Can you spot an area in your life where your doctrine may be right but your actions wrong? Then take whatever steps are necessary to turn it around.

“But the man who looks intently into the perfect law that gives freedom, and continues to do this, not forgetting what he has heard, but doing it – he will be blessed in what he does.” (Jas. 1:25)

AD 50 | AD 60 | Paul in Rome | AD 70 | AD 80 | AD 90 | Revelation | AD 100

2nd missionary journey
3rd missionary journey
Death of Paul
Death of Nero
Destruction of Jerusalem
Completion of Colosseum in Rome
Destruction of Pompeii and Herculaneum
Death of John

DAY 284 Jesus' teaching

Jesus' teaching about happiness and sorrow
Matthew 8:1, Luke 6:20–26

Treatment of enemies
Luke 6:27–36

Do not judge
Luke 6:37–42

A tree and its fruit
Luke 6:43–45

Wise and foolish builders
Luke 6:46–49

Jesus heals the centurion's servant
Matthew 8:5–13, Luke 7:1–10

He raises a widow's son
Luke 7:11–17

Jesus commends John the Baptist
Luke 7:18–30

Luke 6:46–49

**46"Why do you call me, 'Lord,
Lord,' and do not do what I say?
47I will show you what he is like
who comes to me and hears
my words and puts them into
practice. 48He is like a man building
a house, who dug down deep and
laid the foundation on rock. When
a flood came, the torrent struck
that house but could not shake it,
because it was well built. 49But the
one who hears my words and
does not put them into practice
is like a man who built a house on
the ground without a foundation.
The moment the torrent struck
that house, it collapsed and its
destruction was complete."**

For Thought and **Contemplation**

One of the great laws of the personality is that truth does not become part of a person until they begin acting upon it. Progress from merely assenting to Christ's teachings to fully agreeing with them depends on behaving consistently with them. How good are you at not just listening to His words, but acting on them?

"... Jesus said, 'If you hold to my teaching, you are really my disciples. Then you will know the truth, and the truth will set you free.'" (Jn. 8:31–32)

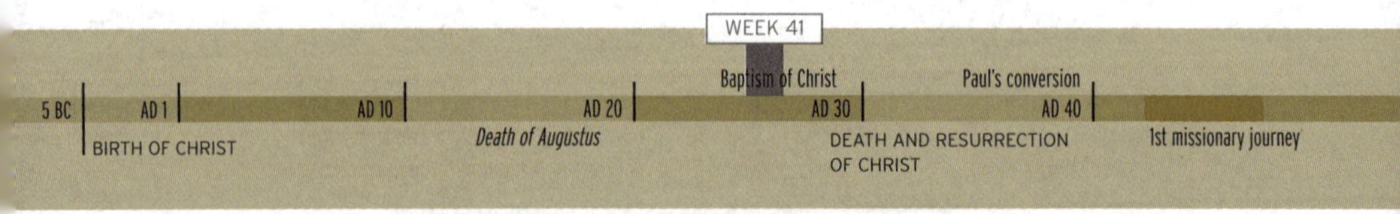

Jesus and Beelzebub

Mark 3:22–27

**[22]And the teachers of the law who
came down from Jerusalem said,
"He is possessed by Beelzebub!
By the prince of demons he is
driving out demons."
[23]So Jesus called them and spoke
to them in parables: "How can
Satan drive out Satan? [24]If a king-
dom is divided against itself, that
kingdom cannot stand. [25]If a house
is divided against itself, that house
cannot stand. [26]And if Satan
opposes himself and is divided, he
cannot stand; his end has come.
[27]In fact, no-one can enter a
strong man's house and carry off
his possessions unless he first ties
up the strong man. Then he can
rob his house.**

Jesus condemns wickedness
Matthew 11:16–19, Luke 7:31–35

The unbelieving towns
Matthew 11:20–24

Invitation to rest
Matthew 11:25–30

Jesus at Simon's home
Luke 7:36–50

The women who accompanied Jesus
Luke 8:1–3

Jesus accused of madness
Mark 3:20–21

Jesus and Beelzebub
Matthew 12:22–30, Mark 3:22–27

The unpardonable sin
Matthew 12:31–37, Mark 3:28–30

The folly of seeking a sign
Matthew 12:38–45

For Thought and **Contemplation**

Just as between Christ and Satan there was no collision or compromise, so it must also be with every one of Christ's followers. If you are for God, then you must be *against* the devil. Check up to see if there are any compromises in your life. And if so, decide right now to do something about them.

"Submit yourselves, then, to God. Resist the devil, and he will flee from you. Come near to God and he will come near to you. ..." (Jas. 4:7–8)

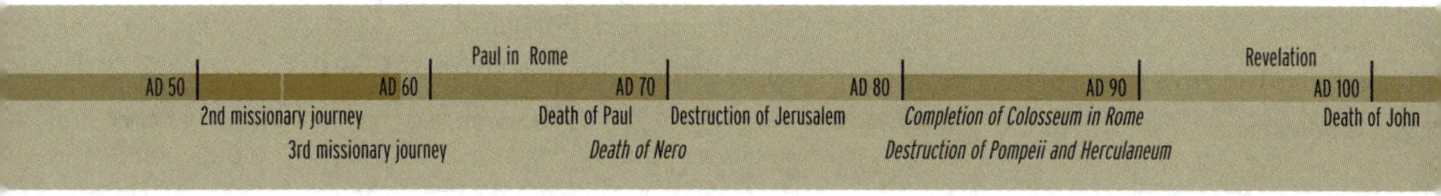

DAY **286** The parables of Jesus

Jesus' mother and brothers
Matthew 12:46–50, Mark 3:31–35, Luke 8:19–21

The parable of the sower
Matthew 13:1–9. Mark 4:1–9, Luke 8:4–8

The purpose of the parables
Matthew 13:10–17, Mark 4:10–12, Luke 8:9–10

The explanation
Matthew 13:18–23, Mark 4:13–20, Luke 8:11–15

A lamp under a bowl
Mark 4:21–25, Luke 8:16–18

The growing seed
Mark 4:26–29

The parable of the weeds
Matthew 13:24–30

Mark 4:26–29

**26He also said, "This is what the
kingdom of God is like. A man
scatters seed on the ground.
27Night and day, whether he sleeps
or gets up, the seed sprouts and
grows, though he does not know
how. 28All by itself the soil produces
corn – first the stalk, then the ear,
then the full grain in the ear. 29As
soon as the grain is ripe, he puts
the sickle to it, because the
harvest has come."**

For Thought and **Contemplation**

In His ministry of teaching, Jesus' goal was never to impress His hearers but to instruct them. How good are you at presenting profound truth with simplicity and directness? Think up a modern parable and then share its truth with someone – today.

"... speaking the truth in love, we will in all things grow up into him who is the Head, that is, Christ." (Eph. 4:15)

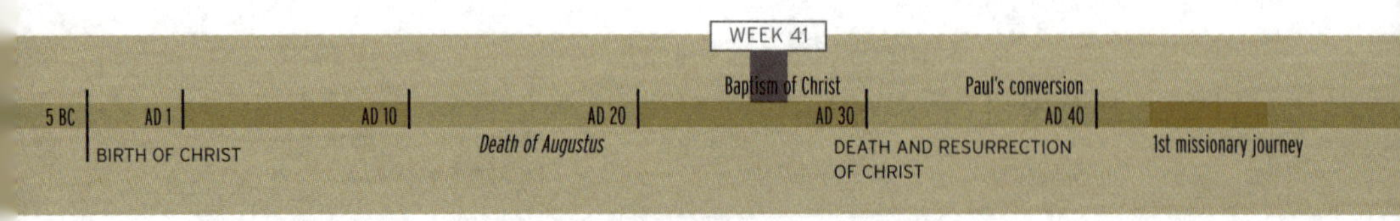

Parables of Jesus

THE PURPOSE of Jesus' parables was to teach in simple, easy-to-understand picture language the message of the kingdom of God. In addition to these, Jesus used epigrams and other memorable sayings, as the Beatitudes and the rest of the Sermon on the Mount show. Jesus used parables so frequently that Mark even says, "[Jesus] did not say anything to them without using a parable" (Mark 4:34).

	Matthew	Mark	Luke
Lamp under a bushel	5:14–15	4:21–22	8:16; 11:33
Houses on rock and on sand	7:24–27		6:47–49
New cloth on an old garment	9:16	2:21	5:36
New wine in old wineskins	9:17	2:23	5:37–38
Sower	13:3–8	4:3–8	8:5–8
The mustard seed	13:31–32	4:30–32	13:18–19
Tares	13:24–30		
Yeast	13:33		13:20–21
Hidden treasure	13:44		
Pearl of great value	13:45–46		
Drag-net	13:47–48		
Lost sheep	18:12–14		15:3–7
Unforgiving servant	18:23–35		
Workers in the vineyard	20:1–16		
Two sons	21:28–31		
Wicked tenants	21:33–41	12:1–9	20:9–16
Invitation to the wedding-feast	22:2–14		
Fig-tree and summer	24:32–33	13:28–29	21:29–32
Ten "bridesmaids"	25:1–13		
Talents/minas	25:14–30		19:12–27
Sheep and goats	25:31–46		
Seedtime to harvest		4:26–29	
Creditor and the debtors			7:41–43
Good Samaritan			10:30–37
Friend in need			11:5–8
Rich fool			12:16–21
Alert servants			12:35–40
Faithful steward			12:42–48
Fig-tree without figs			13:6–9
Wedding-feast			14:7–14
Great banquet			14:16–24
Counting the cost			14:28–33
Lost coin			15:8–10
Prodigal son			15:11–32
Dishonest steward			16:1–8
Rich man and Lazarus			16:19–31
The master and his servant			17:7–10
Persistent widow			18:2–5
Pharisee and the tax collector			18:10–14

DAY 287 More parables

Parables of the mustard seed and the yeast
Matthew 13:31–33, Mark 4:30–32

Jesus' use of parables
Matthew 13:34–35, Mark 4:33–34

Parable of weeds explained
Matthew 13:36–43

Parable of hidden treasure
Matthew 13:44

Parable of the pearl
Matthew 13:45–46

Parable of the net
Matthew 13:47–50

The householder
Matthew 13:51–53

Jesus calms the storm
Matthew 8:18, 23–27, Mark 4:35–41, Luke 8:22–25

Jesus casts out demons
Matthew 8:28–34, Mark 5:1–20

Matthew 13:36–43

**36 Then he left the crowd and went
into the house. His disciples came
to him and said, "Explain to us the
parable of the weeds in the field."
37 He answered, "The one who
sowed the good seed is the Son
of Man. 38 The field is the world,
and the good seed stands for the
sons of the kingdom. The weeds
are the sons of the evil one, 39 and
the enemy who sows them is the
devil. The harvest is the end of
the age, and the harvesters are
angels.
40 "As the weeds are pulled up and
burned in the fire, so it will be at
the end of the age. 41 The Son of
Man will send out his angels, and
they will weed out of his kingdom
everything that causes sin and all
who do evil. 42 They will throw them
into the fiery furnace, where there
will be weeping and gnashing of
teeth. 43 Then the righteous will
shine like the sun in the kingdom
of their Father. He who has ears,
let him hear."**

For Thought and **Contemplation**

Someone has said that Christ's parables are not "bedtime stories to put us to sleep, but bugle calls to wake us up". Has something leapt out from these parables and given you a jolt? Good. Now apply its truth to your life without a moment's delay.

"Do not merely listen to the word, and so deceive yourselves. Do what it says. Anyone who listens to the word but does not do what it says is like a man who looks at his face in a mirror and, after looking at himself, goes away and immediately forgets what he looks like." (Jas. 1:22–24)

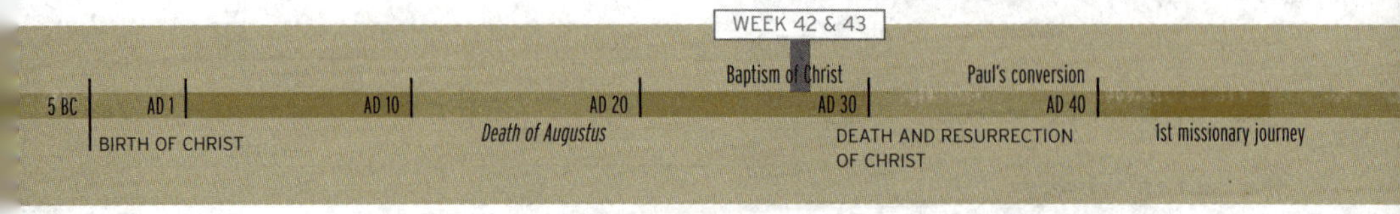

More healings

DAY **288**

Matthew 9:27–34

**27As Jesus went on from there,
two blind men followed him, calling
out, "Have mercy on us, Son of
David!"
28When he had gone indoors, the
blind men came to him, and he
asked them, "Do you believe that
I am able to do this?"
"Yes, Lord," they replied.
29Then he touched their eyes and
said, "According to your faith will
it be done to you"; 30and their sight
was restored. Jesus warned them
sternly, "See that no-one knows
about this." 31But they went out
and spread the news about him all
over that region.
32While they were going out, a
man who was demon-possessed
and could not talk was brought to
Jesus. 33And when the demon was
driven out, the man who had been
mute spoke. The crowd was
amazed and said, "Nothing like
this has ever been seen in Israel."
34But the Pharisees said, "It is by
the prince of demons that he
drives out demons."**

Jesus casts out demons
Luke 8:26–39

The woman who touched Jesus
Matthew 9:18–22, Mark 5:21–34, Luke 8:40–48

Jesus raises Jairus' daughter
Matthew 9:23–26, Mark 5:35–43, Luke 8:49–56

Jesus heals two blind men
Matthew 9:27–31

A dumb man speaks again
Matthew 9:32–34

Jesus rejected again at Nazareth
Matthew 13:54–58, Mark 6:1–6

For Thought and **Contemplation**

The Scripture tells us that "faith comes by hearing, and hearing by the word of God" (Romans 10:17, NKJ). Is there a physical or psychological problem in your life that, despite any help you have received, refuses to budge? Then, with renewed faith, ask Him to make this the day of your deliverance.

"Now faith is being sure of what we hope for and certain of what we do not see." (Heb. 11:1)

AD 50 | AD 60 | AD 70 | AD 80 | AD 90 | AD 100

2nd missionary journey
3rd missionary journey
Paul in Rome
Death of Paul
Death of Nero
Destruction of Jerusalem
Completion of Colosseum in Rome
Destruction of Pompeii and Herculaneum
Revelation
Death of John

The mission of the twelve

Jesus sends out the twelve disciples
Matthew 9:35–38, 10:1–4, Luke 9:1–2

His instructions to them
Matthew 10:5–15, Mark 6:7–11, Luke 9:3–5

The persecution of the disciples
Matthew 10:16–33

The cost and rewards of discipleship
Matthew 10:34–42, 11:1, Mark 6:12–13, Luke 9:6

Death of John the Baptist AD 27

Death of John the Baptist
Matthew 14:1–12, Mark 6:14–29, Luke 9:7–9

Mark 6:7–11

**7Calling the Twelve to him, he sent
them out two by two and gave
them authority over evil spirits.
8These were his instructions:
"Take nothing for the journey
except a staff - no bread, no bag,
no money in your belts. 9Wear
sandals but not an extra tunic.
10Whenever you enter a house,
stay there until you leave that
town. 11And if any place will not
welcome you or listen to you,
shake the dust off your feet when
you leave, as a testimony against
them."**

For Thought and Contemplation

What a challenge Christ presented to those twelve disciples when He told them to go and do exactly as He had done. But then, as someone has said, "No one has ever tested the resources of God until they come up against that which is humanly impossible."

"I can do everything through him who gives me strength." (Phil. 4:13)

a bird's eye view of Matthew

Place in the Bible	Written by:	Special Features
First New Testament book; first Gospel.	Matthew.	Five distinct sections record the teaching of Jesus: the Sermon on the Mount (5–7), the Twelve being sent out (10), parables about the Kingdom (13), teaching about discipleship (18), and the coming kingdom (24–25).

The feeding of the five thousand

Matthew 14:13–19

[13]When Jesus heard what had
happened, he withdrew by boat
privately to a solitary place.
Hearing of this, the crowds
followed him on foot from the
towns. [14]When Jesus landed and
saw a large crowd, he had
compassion on them and healed
their sick.
[15]As evening approached, the
disciples came to him and said,
"This is a remote place, and it's
already getting late. Send the
crowds away, so that they can go
to the villages and buy themselves
some food."
[16]Jesus replied, "They do not need
to go away. You give them some-
thing to eat."
[17]"We have here only five loaves
of bread and two fish," they
answered.
[18]"Bring them here to me," he
said. [19]And he directed the people
to sit down on the grass. Taking
the five loaves and the two fish
and looking up to heaven, he gave
thanks and broke the loaves. Then
he gave them to the disciples, and
the disciples gave them to the
people.

The feeding of the five thousand
Matthew 14:13–21, Mark 6:30–44, Luke 9:10–17, John 6:1–13

Jesus leaves the crowd
Matthew 14:22–23, Mark 6:45–46, John 6:14–15

Jesus walks on the water
Matthew 14:24–33, Mark 6:47–52, John 6:16–21

He heals the sick at Gennesaret
Matthew 14:34–36, Mark 6:53–56

For Thought and **Contemplation**

"A miracle," said C.S. Lewis, "is God taking the ordinary processes of nature and *speeding them up*." Normally, nature takes several seasons to make bread; the wheat, the grain, the flour etc. But what nature takes seasons to do, Christ did in seconds. Carry with you into the day the thrilling fact that God is so much greater than the world He has made.

"Jesus looked at them and said, 'With man this is impossible, but with God all things are possible.'" (Matt. 19:26)

Jesus and the Book

Quoting the Old Testament sixty-five times, Matthew shows how Jesus fulfils the prophecies about the promised Messiah culminating in His death and resurrection from the dead. Out of Matthew's 1,071 verses, 60 per cent are the spoken words of Jesus.

Teaching

Matthew presents Jesus as "King of the Jews" at His birth (Matt. 2:2) and His death (Matt. 27:37). His aim is to show the real nature of His Kingdom, especially in the parables. The Gospel closes with Jesus' command "to make disciples of all nations." (Matt. 28:19)

A Verse to Remember

"You are the Christ, the Son of the living God" (Matt. 16:16).

DAY **291** The bread of life

The people seek Jesus
John 6:22–24

Jesus teaches about spiritual food
John 6:25–33

Jesus, the bread of life
John 6:34–59

Many disciples desert Jesus
John 6:60–71

The hypocrisy of the scribes and Pharisees
Matthew 15:1–9, Mark 7:1–13

Things that make a person unclean
Matthew 15:10–20, Mark 7:14–23

John 6:34–40

**34“Sir,” they said, “from now on
give us this bread.”
35Then Jesus declared, “I am the
bread of life. He who comes to me
will never go hungry, and he who
believes in me will never be thirsty.
36But as I told you, you have seen
me and still you do not believe.
37All that the Father gives me will
come to me, and whoever comes
to me I will never drive away. 38For
I have come down from heaven
not to do my will but to do the will
of him who sent me. 39And this is
the will of him who sent me, that
I shall lose none of all that he has
given me, but raise them up at the
last day. 40For my Father’s will is
that everyone who looks to the
Son and believes in him shall have
eternal life, and I will raise him up
at the last day.”**

For Thought and **Contemplation**

How true it is that, although thousands follow Christ when He gives them what they want, few are prepared to follow Him when He confronts them with what *He* wants. Check up on your own discipleship today. Are you more concerned with what you want, or what *He* wants?

“If you love me, you will obey what I command.” (Jn. 14:15)

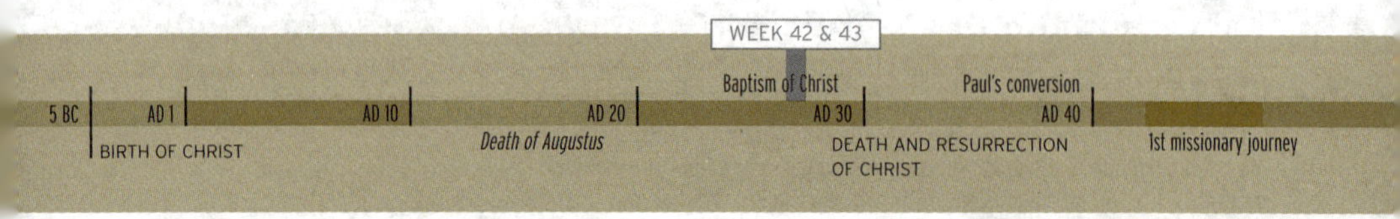

Peter's momentous confession

Matthew 16:13–20

13When Jesus came to the region
of Caesarea Philippi, he asked his
disciples, "Who do people say the
Son of Man is?"
14They replied, "Some say John
the Baptist; others say Elijah; and
still others, Jeremiah or one of the
prophets."
15"But what about you?" he asked.
"Who do you say I am?"
16Simon Peter answered, "You are
the Christ, the Son of the living
God."
17Jesus replied, "Blessed are you,
Simon son of Jonah, for this was
not revealed to you by man, but by
my Father in heaven.
18And I tell
you that you are Peter, and on this
rock I will build my church, and the
gates of Hades will not overcome
it.
19I will give you the keys of the
kingdom of heaven; whatever you
bind on earth will be bound in
heaven, and whatever you loose
on earth will be loosed in heaven."
20Then he warned his disciples not
to tell anyone that he was the
Christ.

The Syro-Phoenician woman
Matthew 15:21–28, Mark 7:24–30

Jesus heals many
Matthew 15:29–31, Mark 7:31–37

Jesus feeds the four thousand
Matthew 15:32–38, Mark 8:1–9

The demand for a sign
Matthew 15:39, 16:1–4, Mark 8:10–12

The yeast of the Pharisees and Sadducees
Matthew 16:5–12, Mark 8:13–21

Jesus heals a blind man
Mark 8:22–26

Peter's declaration
Matthew 16:13–20

For Thought and **Contemplation**

Do you sometimes find yourself doing what Simon Peter did – one moment listening to the voice of God (Matt. 16:16), the next moment listening to the voice of Satan? (Matt. 16:22) Remember, although you may not be able to avoid hearing Satan's voice, you can most certainly decide to resist him.

"Be self-controlled and alert. Your enemy the devil prowls around like a roaring lion looking for someone to devour. Resist him, standing firm in the faith ..." (1 Pet. 5:8–9)

AD 50 | AD 60 | AD 70 | AD 80 | AD 90 | AD 100
2nd missionary journey
3rd missionary journey
Paul in Rome
Death of Paul
Death of Nero
Destruction of Jerusalem
Completion of Colosseum in Rome
Destruction of Pompeii and Herculaneum
Revelation
Death of John

Peter's declaration
Mark 8:27–30, Luke 9:18–21

Jesus speaks of His suffering and death
Matthew 16:21–23, Mark 8:31–33, Luke 9:22

Jesus speaks about self-denial
Matthew 16:24–28, Mark 8:34–38, 9:1, Luke 9:23–27

The transfiguration
Matthew 17:1–8, Mark 9:2–8, Luke 9:28–36

Question about Elijah
Matthew 17:9–13, Mark 9:9–13

Jesus' ministry of healing and deliverance
Matthew 17:14–21

Luke 9:28–36

**[28]About eight days after Jesus
said this, he took Peter, John and
James with him and went up onto
a mountain to pray. [29]As he was
praying, the appearance of his
face changed, and his clothes
became as bright as a flash of
lightning. [30]Two men, Moses and
Elijah, [31]appeared in glorious
splendour, talking with Jesus. They
spoke about his departure, which
he was about to bring to fulfilment
at Jerusalem. [32]Peter and his
companions were very sleepy,
but when they became fully
awake, they saw his glory and the
two men standing with him. [33]As
the men were leaving Jesus, Peter
said to him, "Master, it is good for
us to be here. Let us put up three
shelters – one for you, one for
Moses and one for Elijah." (He did
not know what he was saying.)
[34]While he was speaking, a cloud
appeared and enveloped them,
and they were afraid as they
entered the cloud. [35]A voice came
from the cloud, saying, "This is my
Son, whom I have chosen; listen
to him." [36]When the voice had
spoken, they found that Jesus
was alone. ...**

For Thought and **Contemplation**

G. Campbell Morgan points out that, according to Luke, Jesus did not go up the mountain to be transfigured – He went up to pray. Prayer was the goal, transfiguration the result. You just cannot predict the outcome of a time of prayer with the Lord. Who knows what will result from your own prayer time today!

"When you pray, go into your room, close the door and pray to your Father, who is unseen. Then your Father, who sees what is done in secret, will reward you." (Matt. 6:6)

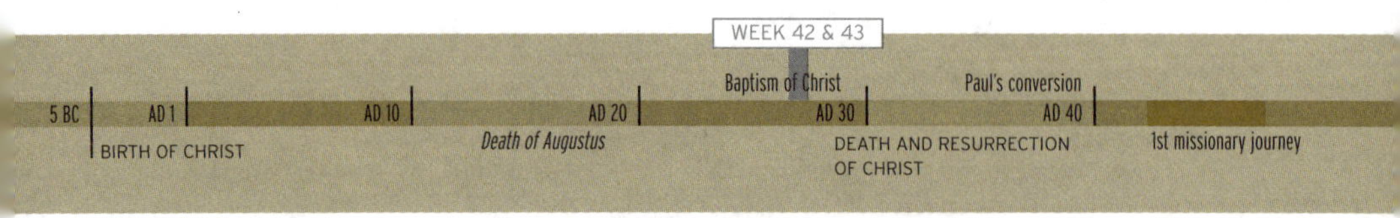

Who's the greatest?

Mark 9:33–37

33They came to Capernaum. When
he was in the house, he asked
them, "What were you arguing
about on the road?" 34But they
kept quiet because on the way
they had argued about who was
the greatest.
35Sitting down, Jesus called the
Twelve and said, "If anyone wants
to be first, he must be the very
last, and the servant of all."
36He took a little child and had him
stand among them. Taking him in
his arms, he said to them,
37"Whoever welcomes one of
these little children in my name
welcomes me; and whoever
welcomes me does not welcome
me but the one who sent me."

Jesus' ministry of healing and deliverance
Mark 9:14–29, Luke 9:37–43

Jesus speaks again about His death
Matthew 17:22–23, Mark 9:30–32, Luke 9:44–45

Payment of the Temple tax
Matthew 17:24–27

Who's the greatest?
Matthew 18:1–5, Mark 9:33–37, Luke 9:46–48

Causes of sin
Matthew 18:6–9, Mark 9:42–50

The parable of the lost sheep
Matthew 18:10–14

John is rebuked
Mark 9:38–41, Luke 9:49–50

Teaching on forgiveness and prayer
Matthew 18:15–20

For Thought and **Contemplation**

How do you view spiritual greatness? Being a leader? Lording it over others? That is not greatness; that is smallness. Greatness is the ability to *serve* others, not control them, and that comes only through a right view of God, yourself and others. How much time do you need to spend on improving your "serve"?

"The greatest among you will be your servant. For whoever exalts himself will be humbled, and whoever humbles himself will be exalted." (Matt. 23:11–12)

AD 50 | AD 60 | AD 70 | AD 80 | AD 90 | AD 100

2nd missionary journey
3rd missionary journey
Paul in Rome
Death of Paul
Death of Nero
Destruction of Jerusalem
Completion of Colosseum in Rome
Destruction of Pompeii and Herculaneum
Revelation
Death of John

DAY **295**

An unforgiving spirit

The parable of the unforgiving servant
Matthew 18:21–35

Jesus' unbelieving brothers
John 7:1–9

Jesus at the Feast of Tabernacles
John 7:10–13

He teaches in the Temple
John 7:14–31

Guards sent to arrest Him
John 7:32–36

The water of life
John 7:37–39

The dispute
John 7:40–53

The woman caught in adultery
John 8:1–11

The light of the world
John 8:12–20

John 7:37–39

**37 On the last and greatest day of
the Feast, Jesus stood and said in
a loud voice, "If anyone is thirsty,
let him come to me and drink.
38 Whoever believes in me, as the
Scripture has said, streams of
living water will flow from within
him." 39 By this he meant the Spirit,
whom those who believed in him
were later to receive. Up to that
time the Spirit had not been given,
since Jesus had not yet been
glorified.**

For Thought and **Contemplation**

One of the most terrible effects of an unforgiving spirit is that it interferes with one's own spiritual assurance. "He who does not offer forgiveness to others," said someone, "destroys the bridge over which God's forgiveness passes to his own heart." Solemn words. Write them on your heart today.

"Be kind and compassionate to one another, forgiving each other, just as in Christ God forgave you." (Eph. 4:32)

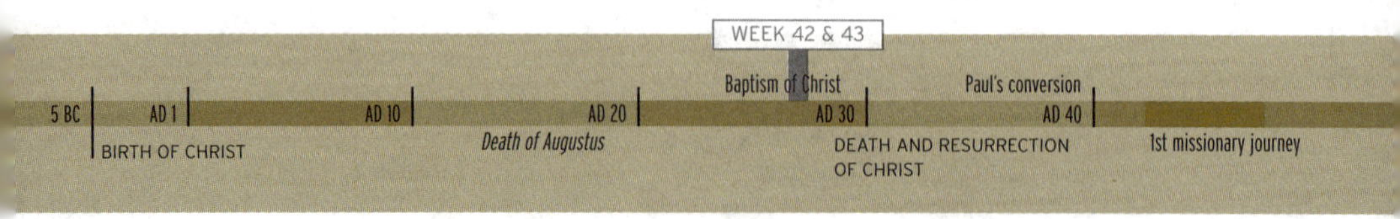

The return of the seventy

DAY **296**

Luke 10:21–24

21At that time Jesus, full of joy
through the Holy Spirit, said, "I
praise you, Father, Lord of heaven
and earth, because you have
hidden these things from the wise
and learned, and revealed them to
little children. Yes, Father, for this
was your good pleasure.
22"All things have been committed
to me by my Father. No-one
knows who the Son is except the
Father, and no-one knows who the
Father is except the Son and
those to whom the Son chooses
to reveal him."
23Then he turned to his disciples
and said privately, "Blessed are
the eyes that see what you see.
24For I tell you that many prophets
and kings wanted to see what you
see but did not see it, and to hear
what you hear but did not hear it."

Jesus and the Jewish authorities
John 8:21–30

Spiritual freedom
John 8:31–38

Sons of Abraham
John 8:39–41

Children of the devil
John 8:42–47

The claims of Jesus
John 8:48–59

Samaritan opposition
Luke 9:51–56

The cost of following Jesus
Matthew 8:19–22, Luke 9:57–62

Jesus sends out the seventy
Luke 10:1–12

The unbelieving towns
Luke 10:13–16

The return of the seventy
Luke 10:17–20

Jesus' joy
Luke 10:21–24

For Thought and **Contemplation**

What is *your* greatest reason for rejoicing? That your prayers are answered? That devils are subject to you in Jesus' Name? That you are a successful Christian? Our *greatest* reason for rejoicing is the fact that our names are written in heaven (Luke 10:20). Spend as much time as you can today thanking your heavenly Father for this stupendous fact!

"... the rest of my fellow-workers, whose names are in the book of life. Rejoice in the Lord always. I will say it again: Rejoice!" (Phil. 4:3–4)

AD 50 | AD 60 | AD 70 | AD 80 | AD 90 | AD 100

2nd missionary journey
3rd missionary journey
Paul in Rome
Death of Paul
Death of Nero
Destruction of Jerusalem
Completion of Colosseum in Rome
Destruction of Pompeii and Herculaneum
Revelation
Death of John

The Good Shepherd

The parable of the good Samaritan
Luke 10:25–37

Jesus visits Martha and Mary
Luke 10:38–42

The healing of the man born blind
John 9:1–41

The parable of the shepherd
John 10:1–6

Jesus, the Good Shepherd
John 10:7–21

Jesus at the Feast of Dedication
John 10:22–38

Many believe in Him
John 10:39–42

John 10:1–6

**1"I tell you the truth, the man who
does not enter the sheep pen by
the gate, but climbs in by some
other way, is a thief and a robber.
2The man who enters by the gate
is the shepherd of his sheep. 3The
watchman opens the gate for him,
and the sheep listen to his voice.
He calls his own sheep by name
and leads them out. 4When he has
brought out all his own, he goes
on ahead of them, and his sheep
follow him because they know his
voice. 5But they will never follow a
stranger; in fact, they will run
away from him because they do
not recognise a stranger's voice."
6Jesus used this figure of speech,
but they did not understand what
he was telling them.**

For Thought and **Contemplation**

The words, "I am the Good Shepherd", are not a figure of speech; they show that Christ is a loving and concerned protector of His children. Are you overcome with worry and despair? Do you find it difficult to get to sleep at night? Then perhaps, instead of counting sheep, you might try talking to the Shepherd!

"The Lord is my shepherd, I shall not be in want. He makes me lie down in green pastures, he leads me beside quiet waters." (Psa. 23:1–2)

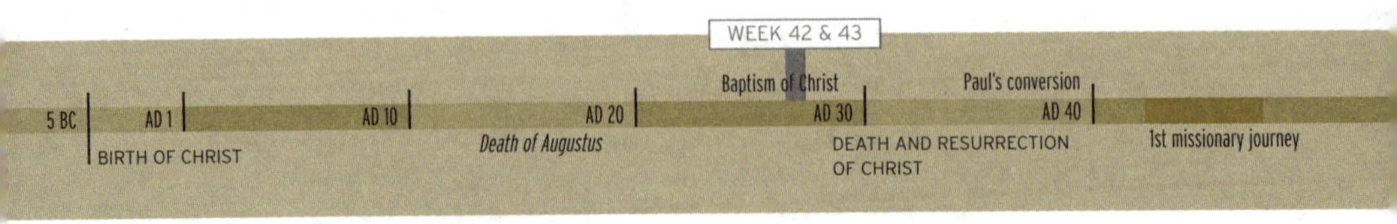

Warnings and encouragements

DAY **298**

Luke 12:4–7

**4"I tell you, my friends, do not be
afraid of those who kill the body
and after that can do no more.
5But I will show you whom you
should fear: Fear him who, after
the killing of the body, has power
to throw you into hell. Yes, I tell
you, fear him. 6Are not five spar-
rows sold for two pennies? Yet not
one of them is forgotten by God.
7Indeed, the very hairs of your
head are all numbered. Don't be
afraid; you are worth more than
many sparrows."**

Jesus' teaching on prayer
Luke 11:1–13

His teaching on Satan's kingdom
Luke 11:14–26

True happiness
Luke 11:27–28

The demand for a miracle
Luke 11:29–32

The light of the body
Luke 11:33–36

Blind guides
Luke 11:37–54

Warning against hypocrisy
Luke 12:1–3

God's care
Luke 12:4–7

Confession or rejection
Luke 12:8–12

The parable of the rich fool
Luke 12:13–21

Trust in God
Luke 12:22–31

Treasure in heaven
Luke 12:32–34

For Thought and **Contemplation**

Recent studies show that millions of people suffer from a low sense of worth. Many feel that they are just names on a computer, or numbers on a card. But in God's sight, every human being is of priceless value. Write out Luke 12:7 on a card and read it at least a dozen times today!

"Your eyes saw my unformed body. All the days ordained for me were written in your book before one of them came to be. How precious to me are your thoughts, O God! How vast is the sum of them!" (Psa. 139:16–17)

AD 50 | AD 60 | AD 70 | AD 80 | AD 90 | AD 100

2nd missionary journey
3rd missionary journey
Paul in Rome
Death of Paul
Death of Nero
Destruction of Jerusalem
Completion of Colosseum in Rome
Destruction of Pompeii and Herculaneum
Revelation
Death of John

DAY **299** The kingdom of God

Watchful servants
Luke 12:35–40

Faithful and unfaithful servants
Luke 12:41–48

Jesus, the cause of division
Luke 12:49–53

Interpreting the times
Luke 12:54–59

Repent or perish
Luke 13:1–5

The unfruitful fig tree
Luke 13:6–9

Jesus heals on the Sabbath
Luke 13:10–17

Parables about the kingdom of God
Luke 13:18–21

The narrow door
Luke 13:22–30

Jesus' love for Jerusalem
Luke 13:31–35

Jesus heals a sick man
Luke 14:1–6

Humility and hospitality
Luke 14:7–14

Luke 14:1–6

**1One Sabbath, when Jesus went
to eat in the house of a prominent
Pharisee, he was being carefully
watched. 2There in front of him
was a man suffering from dropsy.
3Jesus asked the Pharisees and
experts in the law, "Is it lawful to
heal on the Sabbath or not?" 4But
they remained silent. So taking
hold of the man, he healed him
and sent him away.
5Then he asked them, "If one of
you has a son or an ox that falls
into a well on the Sabbath day, will
you not immediately pull him out?"
6And they had nothing to say.**

For Thought and **Contemplation**

Has it ever occurred to you, as you read the account of Christ's ministry on earth, that He seemed to have little or no concern for His own personal needs? Perhaps it was because, as Hudson Taylor so eloquently said, "God's work done in God's way will never lack God's supply."

"But seek first his kingdom and his righteousness, and all these things will be given to you as well." (Matt. 6:33)

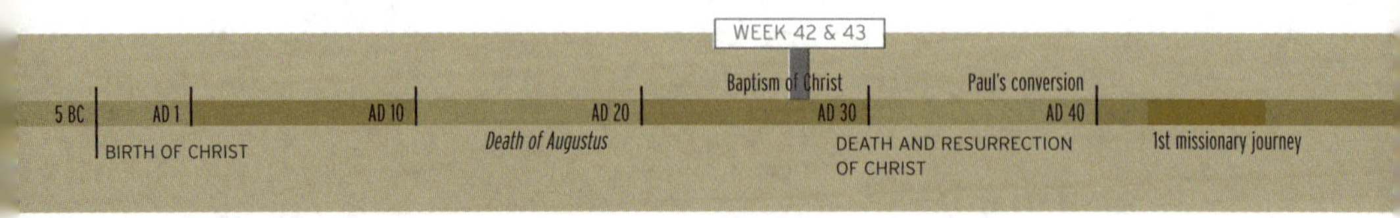

Palestine in the time of Jesus

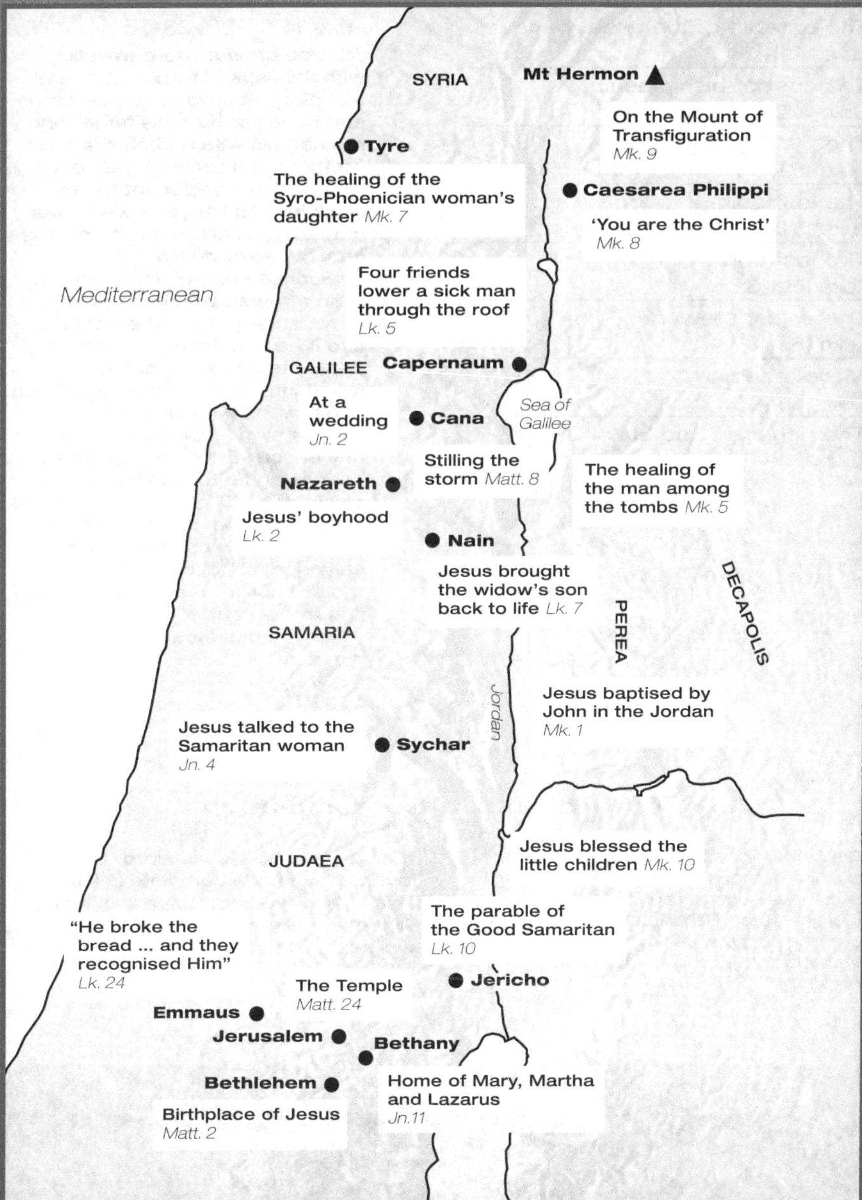

DAY **300** The challenge of discipleship

The parable of the great banquet
Luke 14:15–24

The cost of discipleship
Luke 14:25–35

The lost sheep
Luke 15:1–7

The lost coin
Luke 15:8–10

The lost son
Luke 15:11–32

The unjust steward
Luke 16:1–13

More teaching
Luke 16:14–18

The rich man and Lazarus
Luke 16:19–31

Luke 14:25–29, 33–35

**25Large crowds were travelling
with Jesus, and turning to them
he said: 26"If anyone comes to me
and does not hate his father and
mother, his wife and children, his
brothers and sisters - yes, even
his own life - he cannot be my
disciple. 27And anyone who does
not carry his cross and follow me
cannot be my disciple.
28"Suppose one of you wants to
build a tower. Will he not first sit
down and estimate the cost to
see if he has enough money to
complete it? 29For if he lays the
foundation and is not able to finish
it, everyone who sees it will
ridicule him ... 33In the same way,
any of you who does not give up
everything he has cannot be my
disciple.
34"Salt is good, but if it loses its
saltiness, how can it be made
salty again? 35It is fit neither for
the soil nor for the manure heap;
it is thrown out.
"He who has ears to hear, let
him hear."**

For Thought and **Contemplation**

The Christian Church is desperately in need of a new definition of discipleship. The word has become smudged and discoloured through years of misuse. Read again the meaning of discipleship as presented by Christ in Luke 14:25–35 and ask yourself: Am I truly His disciple?

"... if anyone obeys his word, God's love is truly made complete in him. This is how we know we are in him: Whoever claims to live in him must walk as Jesus did." (1 Jn 2:5–6)

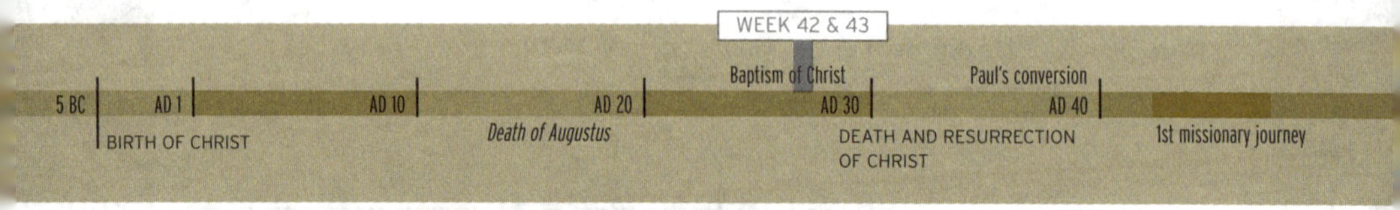

The resurrection and the life

John 11:17–27

**[17]On his arrival, Jesus found that
Lazarus had already been in the
tomb for four days. [18]Bethany was
less than two miles from
Jerusalem, [19]and many Jews had
come to Martha and Mary to
comfort them in the loss of their
brother. [20]When Martha heard that
Jesus was coming, she went out
to meet him, but Mary stayed at
home.**
**[21]"Lord," Martha said to Jesus,
"if you had been here, my brother
would not have died. [22]But I know
that even now God will give you
whatever you ask."**
**[23]Jesus said to her, "Your brother
will rise again."**
**[24]Martha answered, "I know he
will rise again in the resurrection
at the last day."**
**[25]Jesus said to her, "I am the
resurrection and the life. He who
believes in me will live, even
though he dies; [26]and whoever
lives and believes in me will never
die. Do you believe this?"**
**[27]"Yes, Lord," she told him, "I
believe that you are the Christ, the
Son of God, who was to come into
the world."**

The unprofitable servant
Luke 17:1–10

The death of Lazarus
John 11:1–16

Jesus the resurrection and the life
John 11:17–27

Jesus weeps
John 11:28–37

The raising of Lazarus
John 11:38–44

The plot against Jesus
John 11:45–53

Jesus goes to Ephraim
John 11:54

The healing of the ten lepers
Luke 17:11–19

The coming of the kingdom of God
Luke 17:20–37

For Thought and **Contemplation**

Have you ever realised that Jesus did not say, "I am the resurrection and the life" after He rose from the dead, but prior to it? What does this imply? It implies that Jesus was not the Resurrection because He rose from the dead, but He rose from the dead because He was the Resurrection.

"And if the Spirit of him who raised Jesus from the dead is living in you, he who raised Christ from the dead will also give life to your mortal bodies through his Spirit, who lives in you." (Rom. 8:11)

AD 50 | AD 60 | AD 70 | AD 80 | AD 90 | AD 100

2nd missionary journey
3rd missionary journey
Paul in Rome
Death of Paul
Death of Nero
Destruction of Jerusalem
Completion of Colosseum in Rome
Destruction of Pompeii and Herculaneum
Revelation
Death of John

DAY **302** Jesus and divorce

The parable of the persistent widow
Luke 18:1–8

The parable of the Pharisee and the tax collector
Luke 18:9–14

Jesus' teaching about divorce
Matthew 19:1–12, Mark 10:1–12

He blesses little children
Matthew 19:13–15, Mark 10:13–16, Luke 18:15–17

The rich young ruler
Matthew 19:16–30, Mark 10:17–31

Mark 10:2–12

[2]Some Pharisees came and test-
ed him by asking, "Is it lawful for a
man to divorce his wife?"
[3]"What did Moses command
you?" he replied.
[4]They said, "Moses permitted
a man to write a certificate of
divorce and send her away."
[5]"It was because your hearts
were hard that Moses wrote you
this law," Jesus replied. [6]"But at
the beginning of creation God
'made them male and female.'
[7]'For this reason a man will leave
his father and mother and be
united to his wife, [8]and the two will
become one flesh.' So they are no
longer two, but one. [9]Therefore
what God has joined together, let
man not separate."
[10]When they were in the house
again, the disciples asked Jesus
about this. [11]He answered,
"Anyone who divorces his wife
and marries another woman
commits adultery against her.
[12]And if she divorces her husband
and marries another man, she
commits adultery."

For Thought and **Contemplation**

How do you feel about divorce? God says in the Old Testament that He *hates* it (Mal. 2:16). Britain has a reputation of having one of the highest divorce rates in Europe. Spend a few minutes in prayer today asking God what He would have you do to help stop the break-up of homes and families.

"... God was reconciling the world to himself in Christ, not counting men's sins against them. And he has committed to us the message of reconciliation." (2 Cor. 5:19)

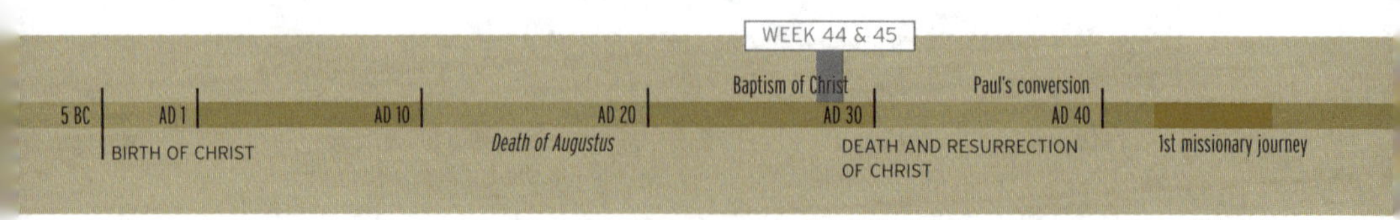

The over-ambitious disciples

Mark 10:35–40, 43–45

**35Then James and John, the sons
of Zebedee, came to him.
"Teacher," they said, "we want
you to do for us whatever we
ask."
36"What do you want me to do for
you?" he asked.
37They replied, "Let one of us sit
at your right and the other at your
left in your glory."
38"You don't know what you are
asking," Jesus said. "Can you
drink the cup I drink or be baptised
with the baptism I am baptised
with?"
39"We can," they answered.
Jesus said to them, "You will drink
the cup I drink and be baptised
with the baptism I am baptised
with, 40but to sit at my right or left
is not for me to grant. These
places belong to those for whom
they have been prepared." ...
43"Not so with you. Instead, who-
ever wants to become great
among you must be your servant,
44and whoever wants to be first
must be slave of all. 45For even the
Son of Man did not come to be
served, but to serve, and to give
his life as a ransom for many."**

The rich young ruler
Luke 18:18–30

The parable of the workers in the vineyard
Matthew 20:1–16

Jesus speaks of the crucifixion
Matthew 20:17–19, Mark 10:32–34, Luke 18:31–34

The ambition of James and John
Matthew 20:20–28, Mark 10:35–45

The two blind men healed
Matthew 20:29–34

Blind Bartimaeus is healed
Mark 10:46–52, Luke 18:35–43

For Thought and **Contemplation**

How did Jesus deal with problem people in His life, such as His over-ambitious disciples? He turned every problem into a possibility by using it as an opportunity to drive home some new and vital spiritual truth. Put this principle to work in your own life, and it will mean all the difference between success and failure in your relationships.

"A man finds joy in giving an apt reply – and how good is a timely word!" (Prov. 15:23)

AD 50 | AD 60 | Paul in Rome | AD 70 | AD 80 | AD 90 | Revelation | AD 100

2nd missionary journey
3rd missionary journey
Death of Paul
Death of Nero
Destruction of Jerusalem
Completion of Colosseum in Rome
Destruction of Pompeii and Herculaneum
Death of John

The triumphal entry

The conversion of Zacchaeus
Luke 19:1–10

The parable of the gold coins
Luke 19:11–27

Jesus arrives at Bethany
John 11:55–57, 12:1

The plot against Lazarus
John 12:9–11

Jesus is anointed at Bethany
John 12:2–8

The triumphant entry into Jerusalem
Matthew 21:1–11, Mark 11:1–11, Luke 19:28–44, John 12:12–19

John 12:12–18

12 The next day the great crowd
that had come for the Feast heard
that Jesus was on his way to
Jerusalem. 13 They took palm
branches and went out to meet
him, shouting,
"Hosanna!"
"Blessed is he who comes in the
name of the Lord!"
"Blessed is the King of Israel!"
14 Jesus found a young donkey and
sat upon it, as it is written,
15 "Do not be afraid, O Daughter
of Zion;
see, your king is coming,
seated on a donkey's colt."
16 At first his disciples did not
understand all this. Only after
Jesus was glorified did they
realise that these things had been
written about him and that they
had done these things to him.
17 Now the crowd that was with
him when he called Lazarus from
the tomb and raised him from the
dead continued to spread the
word. 18 Many people, because
they had heard that he had given
this miraculous sign, went out to
meet him.

For Thought and **Contemplation**

Human nature is such that, on one day, it can receive Christ with palms and rejoicing, and the next day send Him to a cross. Multitudes of people admire Christ, but few become consistent disciples. How about you? Are you just one of Christ's admirers – or a true disciple?

"Dear children, let us not love with words or tongue but with actions and in truth." (1 Jn. 3:18)

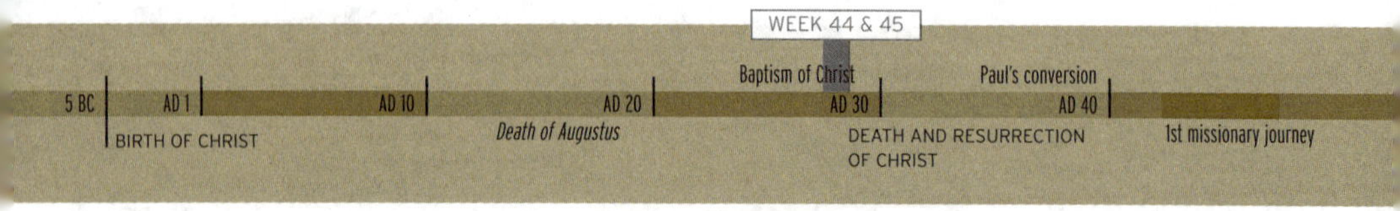

Jesus' authority

Matthew 21:23–27

23Jesus entered the temple courts, and, while he was teaching, the chief priests and the elders of the people came to him. "By what authority are you doing these things?" they asked. "And who gave you this authority?"

24Jesus replied, "I will also ask you one question. If you answer me, I will tell you by what authority I am doing these things. 25John's baptism – where did it come from? Was it from heaven, or from men?"

They discussed it among themselves and said, "If we say, 'From heaven,' he will ask, 'Then why didn't you believe him?' 26But if we say, 'From men' – we are afraid of the people, for they all hold that John was a prophet."

27So they answered Jesus, "We don't know."

Then he said, "Neither will I tell you by what authority I am doing these things."

Second cleansing of Temple
Matthew 21:12–17, Mark 11:15–19, Luke 19:45–48

Cursing of the fig tree
Matthew 21:18–19, Mark 11:12–14

The fig tree withers
Matthew 21:20–22, Mark 11:20–25

Jesus' authority is challenged
Matthew 21:23–27, Mark 11:27–33, Luke 20:1–8

The parable of the two sons
Matthew 21:28–32

The parable of the wicked tenants
Matthew 21:33–46, Mark 12:1–12, Luke 20:9–19

For Thought and **Contemplation**

The authority of Christ is still questioned today – even by Christians! Someone has said there are usually three reactions given to Christ's words – inattention, irritation or instant obedience. Which of these three reactions is characteristic of your response to Christ's words?

"Whoever has my commands and obeys them, he is the one who loves me. He who loves me will be loved by my Father, and I too will love him and show myself to him." (John 14:21)

AD 50 | AD 60 | AD 70 | AD 80 | AD 90 | AD 100

2nd missionary journey
3rd missionary journey
Paul in Rome
Death of Paul
Death of Nero
Destruction of Jerusalem
Completion of Colosseum in Rome
Destruction of Pompeii and Herculaneum
Revelation
Death of John

Heart to Heart

Section 10

The wonderful Person of Jesus shines out of the Gospels to heal the sick, comfort the hurt, seek the lost and encourage the faint hearted. You are not just reading about a historical figure but a living Person because Jesus is alive Yesterday, Today and Forever. Praise the name of Jesus.

Visit the web site: **www.cover2cover.org**